A Crack in the Family

A Crack in the Family

Roads Taken Today Determine Your Tomorrows

SISSY B. SMITH

iUniverse, Inc.
Bloomington

A Crack in the Family
Roads Taken Today Determine Your Tomorrows

iUniverse books may be ordered through booksellers or by contacting:

iUniverse
1663 Liberty Drive
Bloomington, IN 47403
www.iuniverse.com
1-800-Authors (1-800-288-4677)

Because of the dynamic nature of the Internet, any Web addresses or links contained in this book may have changed since publication and may no longer be valid. The views expressed in this work are solely those of the author and do not necessarily reflect the views of the publisher, and the publisher hereby disclaims any responsibility for them.

ISBN: 978-1-4502-6978-0 (sc)
ISBN: 978-1-4502-6980-3 (ebook)
ISBN: 978-1-4502-6979-7 (dj)

Library of Congress Control Number: 2010916209

Printed in the United States of America

iUniverse rev. date: 5/27/2011

"In Memory of My Mother and Father"

I want to acknowledge my husband, sons and daughters for all of their support and encouragement; I give special thanks to Shimekka I. Smith, Scherlyn Garnet and Ravin Norfleet for their many hours spent assist me in editing this book.

Table of Contents

Introduction

I was enrolled in college; gainfully employed in changing my future. I felt I had enough on my mind than to be involved with anyone. So when I ran into Kevin, it was a pleasant surprise. We walked, and talked about the past. Soon we were at my sister's (Paula) house. It seemed so normal to walk into the house with him. Just as normal to find myself back in his arms again. After all the years we had been together, he definitely knew my body. I lay back as he caressed me as only he knew how. Kevin took off my clothing with the expertise of a man that knew a woman's body. He expertly took my blouse off with flair. I didn't even know it was off until I felt his warm hands on my breast.

Later I asked Kevin, as I did so many times before, to let me have his child. I also knew, and agreed to the reasons why we should not do this. We both were too young, we both were in college, neither of us had anything to offer a child at this time. We didn't even live in our own apartments. I lived with my sister, and he lived with his grandmother. All that really made sense to me was this could almost certainly be my last chance to get pregnant by him. I so wanted the child of my first love.

He had no idea when my monthly was, like he used to, and he always went "bare back." When he left, I was sure I was pregnant. I hadn't left much room for me not to be. I wanted Kevin's child so I was going to have it, even if I had no intention of letting him in on the miracle of my child's birth. The night I conceived my first child I knew it because I wanted him so much. I didn't see Kevin for awhile, nor did I have anyone else, so I knew when I became pregnant. Kevin didn't want a child, so in my mind, he didn't get one. I would be mother and father to this child. I would be strong enough for both. I would love this child enough for both of us…

The World as I See It; 1951

It was 1951 when *"direct dial, coast-to-coast: telephone[1]"* service began in the United States, the *"Shot Heard 'Round the World[2];"* One of the greatest moments in Major League Baseball history occurred when the New York Giants' Bobby Thomson hit a game winning home run in the bottom of the ninth inning off of the Brooklyn Dodgers' pitcher Ralph Branca, to win the *"National League Pennant[3]"* after being down fourteen games. *"I Love Lucy[4]"* made its television debut on CBS, and *"The Catcher in the Rye[5]"* was first published by J.D. Salinger. The *"Tennessee Williams[6]"* adaptation of A Streetcar Named Desire premiered; becoming a critical and box-office smash. "U.S. *President Harry S. Truman[7]"* relieved *"General Douglas MacArthur[8]"* of his Far Eastern command. The "US *Senate Committee on Armed Services,[9]"* and "U.S. *Senate Committee on Foreign Relations[10]"* began its closed door hearings into the dismissal of General Douglas MacArthur by U.S. President Harry S. Truman, and U.S. President Harry Truman also declared an *"official end to the war[11]"* with Germany during this same year.

I was born in 1951, in a rather large city in the U.S... it really doesn't matter which one. I was the fourth child down, and the baby girl. There were three sisters older, and eight brothers younger, with me between the girls, and boys; in that order. My oldest sister was five years older, and my youngest brother was twelve years my junior. Okay, so I had a large family. It wasn't until 1960 when the birth control pill was approved by the *"Food and Drug Administration[12]"* (FDA), and by 1964 it became the most popular form of birth control. Until then my mother and father had to rely on the birth control available to them. Obviously it wasn't working. I felt my family had a pretty close relationship, with my mother being the rock, and spine of my family. Although she gave birth to so many children, she made each one of us feel special. The Korean War was going on around us but it was never spoken of in my household. My immediate problems consisted of our home life, school days, and what momma was cooking. Daddy's wages were never discussed.

You might say we were poor, but my father was a very proud man. As long as I can remember he worked at a large corporation called, International Harvester. We knew other people doing better, and some doing worse. My father would never think of going on welfare, his pride was so strong; although, I do remember the taste of government cheese, peanut butter, large cans of spam, and sugar with butter sandwiches. Daddy never forgave momma for applying for food distribution, but he couldn't fight her when it came to her children. Momma raised us to love each other and stay together. We made lots of friends throughout our childhood, but no one came near to being considered as close as our siblings were to each other. It was just an unsaid fact of life. We moved around a lot, as I remember. Each new house was a glorious adventure; we had no idea that the rent was due, and we were escaping from the landlord. The shiny glass that held our reality was never broken, at least not at this time of my life. When momma took on a job cleaning houses and washing and ironing clothes for the white folks, she would come home with a smile on her face, and joy in her heart as she went to prepare the dinner we always had on the table.

My mother could cook up a meal with little or nothing, and made a feast of it. When she took on cleaning taverns after they closed, she would bring home packages of peanuts, popcorn, and potato chips. I remember us staying up late for her arrival. I had no idea that Momma had a life other than the one she portrayed to us. She was Momma, and she could do no harm. What momma said was law, everything she did, she did for us.

This was my reality. On the other hand, there was daddy. The proud, strong, strict character that he was, he had a smile that could melt the troubles right off your mind. To hear his laughter when he told a tale, you always wondered if the tale was true or had he just made it up. He could send any one into a fit of laughter right along with him. This side of my daddy, the cheerful strong man, would only come to our house after he changed into his evening attire. He would come home from his job, go straight to his room, closing the door. He worked all day, thinking about changing from the dirty dungarees he wore, into his "going out to check his traps" suits. After work, he would put on his robe, take his bath, and change into one of his three suits. He was so sharp the accessories would look dull in comparison. He'd accessorize with shiny, usually black shoes, and a colorful tie; tied just right. He always placed a matching felt hat on his head.

I don't remember him ever having hair on the top of his head. As the story goes, when my oldest sister, Monica was a little thing when she was young, she would sit on his lap, or on a high chair, I'm not really sure which; spending hours on end trying to braid his hair. She would twist it into so many new hair styles, which is said to be the way he eventually lost the top of his hair. Although Monica was born prior to him meeting, and marrying my mother, he loved her, and treated her as though she was his own. He did have hair on the back, and sides, which he kept neatly trimmed close to his scalp. He smelled of some strong, cheap cologne, Ivory' soap and Old Spice aftershave. He'd stand in front of the full length mirror in his room, which was attached to a movable closet and contained his suits, and shoes.

We were forbidden to go near this closet. Speaking of forbidden areas; my father had a suitcase which he kept under his bed. He would keep old watches, pictures, personal items which he held dear in the suitcase. We were not to touch the suitcase or any of its contents. After assessing himself he would call us to him, this usually being the only time we were allowed to speak to him since his return home. He would model himself in front of us, and always ask, "Do I look good enough to go check my traps now?" We would always agree that he was perfect. Sometimes mama would come out of the kitchen with a smile, and tell him that he needed to straighten his tie, or remove a piece of dust off his suit.

He would be happy that she approved. These were the times when you could see how much my father loved my mother the most. It never occurred to us that checking his traps meant he was going to the taverns to drink, have conversations with his male partners, and his lady friends in the bar. Momma never let on that we should ever feel bad for her, being that she was doomed to watch television, and be home with the children every night. She never seemed happier. These memories of my father were only spiced with a few occasions when we past in the halls or rooms of the house while he prepared to go out on the streets. He returned early in the morning, and dressed for work; departing before we arose to go to school. He sometimes returned home at night so late we were all asleep. I am reminded of the time my teacher told me that I was failing math, so she told me to get with Peter, a young man in my class, and he would help me to understand where we were in math. One day he walked me home, and we were sitting on my porch doing our math homework when my father returned home from work.

When he got out of the car, I could tell he was in a very bad mood. As he got closer to us I could see his eyes, and I had never seen that look on my father's face before. He said to me in a very controlled but heavy voice, "What is this white boy doing on my porch?" I was shocked at the way my father spoke of my friend by his color, so I tried to tell him his name, and how the teacher had said he could help me with my homework. My father said the following, as if he hadn't heard a word I said, "Get that white boy off my porch, and don't you ever bring another one to my house." He said this like I had brought the garbage can from the back, and poured it out on the porch. My friend, like I, was in shock.

When we heard a resounding bellow, come from daddy, "Now!!!" Both of us took off in different directions. Peter ran off the stairs, and down the street. I ran into the house, and to my mother's arms. I'm sure my "use-to-be" friend ran home. I've never been prejudiced, nor have I ever been able to understand how some people can hate others. Especially, the people who really did not do what others did to them. He never spoke to me again. I don't remember anything after that, except my mother's voice trying to get me to understand how my father had his reasons for hating Caucasians. I'm not naïve.

I knew prejudice was still alive, and well in America; it's just that I never looked at my father the same. I don't know whether it was because the hate in his eyes, the fear, and prejudice that he felt or just the fact that he embarrassed me in front of my new friend. I just was unable to forget, or forgive. As I indicated, I was in the middle of the line of children in my family. I was too young to hang with my sisters, yet too old to be with my brothers. At least this is what I told myself as I played in my own little world. My favorite television stars were Judy Garland, Mickey Rooney, and of course, Shirley Temple. I was too shy to go out, and make friends. I would listen to people talk to each other, but I never had anything to offer to the conversations.

I seldom said anything to others. I'd get my baby dolls, and go to a closet, the attic, or even in the basement to live in my own little world. My world would be comprised of my surroundings, and my dolls. I would watch Walt Disney's Alice in Wonderland, and the Mickey Mouse Club, over, and over again. I sometimes would take long walks, in the neighborhood, or sometimes further. No one seemed to miss me, and the further I went the more dramatic my imagination became. I don't remember my parents ever going to the department store, to buy things for me. I wore hand-me-downs such as clothes, and shoes. All of the girls shared socks, and underclothes. We also shared toiletries, soap, and water. The schools never asked us to bring paper, and pens or any of the supplies the schools ask for now. We got up, threw on some clothes, and went to school. We walked to whatever school our parents wanted us to go to. The closest one was usually the chosen one. That is what we called the neighborhood school, store, bar, or church.

I really don't remember my mother or father telling us anything about church or religion. Although I do remember once I came home after talking to my girlfriends about religion. I went home, and told my mother I was going to a catholic church with my friends, Sunday. I got such a negative and powerful reaction to this conversation from my mother; you'd of thought I said I was going to be a devil worshiper. My mother told me, "You're not going to some catholic church! I do not want to hear any more about it." Need I say, "I dropped the subject." If I couldn't go to a church where I wanted to go, I wasn't going to go at all. This seemed to please my mother, and I didn't go to church for about ten years.

What's a Girl to Do; 1963

It was in 1963, people called those years the *"Swinging Sixties,[13]"* and *"Aretha Franklin's[14]"* record "Respect" came out as a hit, 1963 witnessed the *"Beatles[15]"* becoming a big thing, just as was the Rolling Stones, and the *"Ed Sullivan Show[16]."* Our U.S. troops" had the largest offensive of the *"Vietnam War,[17]"* I was twelve years old, and I became a junior high school student. My sisters were within the nine month zone of each other. The exception was Monica, who was five years my senior. The other three of us were pretty much close at least in years. Close enough in age to attend the same schools. Betsy and Paula became running buddies, but as usual I traveled alone. I seldom knew where Betsy or Paula would be. Whether the beginning of school or after school. If they were trying to hide from me, they were doing a great job. Usually the mornings were pretty calm on the way to school. Once the school attendance alarm went off, everyone would run into their designated area for attendance, going into the school building in order.

The journey home was not as controlled, so of course all the children would get together, and do their thing after school. Unfortunately the journey home was usually laced with groups of children that knew each other, whether it be in a good or bad way. Children use to follow me, throw things at me or just call me names, like "Stinky," "Hand-me-down," or "Funky, Funky, Broadway." I would try to ignore them, and continued to walk home, only faster.

There seemed to always be a fight or two after school. Since I remembered, my mother always told us not to stand around and watch the fights; this is why I always turned my head, and walked past them.

Parents didn't walk to or from the schools as they do today, especially with the buses, since we didn't have them. Sometimes I would be home, and I heard how Betsy or Paula had been in one or two of the fights. I never asked them how, or why it happened or even how they were even started. I chose to ignore this side of my life, never telling anyone about it. Years later, I was told by my sisters, "Most of our fights were because of you. Kids, that wanted to fight you, or even if they said something about you, dumbass." Betsy was a small, skinny child, but mean as a rattler. She had earned her reputation of a bully, and not many kids wanted to tangle with her. Paula was a big bone child, as they use to call it. She did not back down from a fight either. So I pretty much believed them when they told me this. I took it as though they loved me and I appreciated their love. Later, I came to realize, they resented my lack of character, and the ability to help myself, or "fight my own battles" as they put it.

I was twelve years old, and in the seventh grade when I got my first introduction into the world of sex. My class was in session, and I was seated next to this pretty girl that sat to my right. There was this guy that sat next to me on my left. I heard him calling Peggy, although she was ignoring him. He kept calling her so finally I looked to see what he was calling her to see. My decision to look was, regrettable, on my part. In his hand he held something between his legs. It seemed to be coming out of his pants. With the reaction I had, you wouldn't believe I had six younger brothers. But I had never seen my brothers like this. It was big, and for some reason it scared me. I immediately looked away, hoping the sight of what I saw would go away. He kept calling Peggy, and asking her if she wanted to sit on it; I raised my hand, and asked the teacher if I could go to the toilet. She said I could, so I got up, and I think I actually ran to the girl's room toilet. Once I got there I got so sick I threw up. That was the first time, but not the last time, I saw an erect penis. I was afraid of that thing boys had in their pants.

I would walk alone to my house every day. I had few friends at this age, as I was still rather quiet. I usually spoke only when spoken too, or when I did speak it was with my head lowered as if I could fend off an insult, or disappear in the event the person I spoke to would say something that would hurt my feelings. The few friends I did have made me laugh, I enjoyed to be with them. To be honest, these friends could say or do just about anything they wished; I wouldn't be offended. I needed their approval, I could not afford to lose the few people that tolerated me, and allowed me to be with them; to call them "my friends."

I had a couple of girls I considered to be my friends. We would walk together before, and after school. Their names were Lawanda Wills, and her cousin, Brenda. Although they lived in the same house, Lawanda lived on the first floor, and Debra the upstairs apartment. Lawanda's mother was Brenda's aunt. Although Lawanda had a serious skin problem, she was beautiful in my eyes. Her hair was always curled perfectly in the same style every day. I've never met anyone, especially with acne like hers, with the confidence in herself that she had. Brenda wasn't beautiful either, but she was nice looking, and what we use to call book smart. She rarely got anything lower than an A for a grade. She wore very thick glasses, and she also kept her hair up. We three practiced for the cheerleading team tryout together, usually at my house. Practice for the tryout was the only time I allowed anyone to come to my house. I knew this was due to the fact that we could do flips in my mother's living room. There was no way we could do it in their beautiful homes. Their house had beautiful furniture, unlike our house. One day I flipped into our living room table, cutting my wrist. I still wear the scar to this day.

Usually I walked from my house to their house, sat at Lawanda's kitchen table waiting for them to get ready for school. I usually carried their school books, especially on cold days. It wasn't like I had to, I would take them when we started walking, and I would just forget I had them. Once we arrived at school, I would give them their books, and we would separate at the school door to go our own way. After school, I would wait at the doors. We would walk to their house first then I would walk to my house alone. Even though we three tried out for the cheerleading team, Lawanda and Debra made it, but I didn't. It was around this time that we stopped walking to, and from school together. I no longer fit into their clique. There was another girl that hung with us sometimes; her name was Patricia Rams. I called her Pat. We would leave their house, walking two blocks up to pick up Pat. She was not pretty. She had long black hair, but she had a pug nose and her teeth extended out from the top over the bottom lip.

8

She was funny though, and sometimes I think the only reason she was in this group was because I liked her. I felt we had more in common, especially the part about not being pretty. She lived with her mother in a small apartment on the way to school. Pat stayed with her mom in a two bedroom apartment. Her mother was single. She had loved a man that considered himself a pimp. He was her pimp, and she led the life of a prostitute until she got pregnant with Pat. This is when he left her. She no longer wanted a man. Pat's mother had many "girlfriends." She also indulged in illegal drugs. I know this because Pat would tell me when no one else was around. She was confused about what her mother was doing. I think she was more concerned about her mother's love life than the drugs.

My First Love; 1967

I was sixteen, in 1967, the world news reported; Medicare began, *"Star Trek[18]"* was big on television. Once Lawanda and Debra began to participate with the other cheerleaders, they would stay late after school, and leave earlier for school because of their practices. Pat and I continued to walk to school, and home together. We were all we had. Later I met a girl named Faith. She was a short white girl with sandy blonde hair. She wasn't particularly pretty but with the heavy layers of make-up she wore, the interested boys would follow her around; starting conversations with her.

In my little world I was so lovesick for this boy named Larry Thomas. Standing about six feet tall, I guess he was around seventeen years old. He had eyes that you could easily float into, and disappear. They were so dreamy, and his skin had such a smooth complexion. His voice was so deep, and sexy; when he spoke I lost all concentration of what I was thinking about, and I felt my stomach come up into my throat; although he seldom spoke to me unless I spoke first to greet him as I walked pass his red brick home.

On my sixteenth birthday, Faith and I were walking home from school. We were discussing boys, in general, and the subject lead to who we liked. I told Faith, "I have a secret love, but if I tell you who it is, you have to keep it a secret between us." "I promised never to tell a soul." I told her, "I love Larry Thomas." I hesitantly added "I've never been kissed by a boy, so I know my chance of getting him to love me is zero."

She was fascinated, "You have got to be lying." This came especially because he happened to be the most popular boy in school. Faith didn't hear anything except his name. She continued with, "All the girls, the socially accepted girls, also have a crush on him." She started laughing so hard she held her stomach, to contain herself. I wished I had never told her. She asked me, "Why don't you just tell him how you feel." I answered, "Are you crazy? How could I, he doesn't even know I'm alive." She said, "How is he going to know you're alive if you don't talk to him? At least talk to him." Around this time, we reached Larry's house, which was situated between the school I attended, and my home. I could have made my route another way but I wouldn't catch a glimpse of him. He was standing outside in his front yard. I have no idea what he was doing there, but as we approached I looked at the man I loved.

Just doing that made my day. Around this time, we reached Larry's house, which was situated between the school I attended, and my home. Just doing that made my day. As we got closer to him, my heart was pounding so hard in my chest, I thought I was about to have a heart attack. Faith ran up to him and with a very sugary voice asked, "Larry, what would you do if you found a girl who had never been kissed at sixteen, and it's her birthday?"

I wanted to fall into the ground. Blood rushed to my head as I realized that she really told him what I had told her in confidence. This was not one promise but two secrets she told him. I wanted to sink into the ground or just die in place. I couldn't run, because I couldn't get my body to obey me. Besides, I didn't know where to run to. I didn't want him to see me acting like a kid. He looked at me with those dreamy eyes, and that beautiful smile. He seemed to just begin to open his mouth to answer her, when I heard a voice behind me. I turned around, and realized it belonged to my cousin, Howard. He had just gotten a car, and he was showing it off. He yelled, "Hey Sis, you guys want a ride home?" I had never been so happy to see Howard. I yelled back, "Yeah, wait up for us." I didn't wait for Larry's answer. As I ran to the car, I grabbed Faith's hand, and pulled her along with me. "Come on Faith." I got into the car never looking back.

Before this, I was so obsessed with Larry; I use to find excuses to walk past his house, hoping he would be in the yard again. He never was. This infatuation eventually ended, but only because I found someone else to love. His name was Carlton. He didn't pay any attention to me either, but at least I got a chance to see him, and be close to him. He was in several of my classes. He was nice though. He never said he knew I liked him. He always spoke to me in class, and in the hallways. It was never about us being together, it was just small talk. I was happy with that. During my teen years, there were several other girls that I befriended. There was Trudy; a pretty girl with a fine shape for a girl her age. She didn't wear makeup, probably due to the fact that she didn't need it. I don't remember Trudy ever hanging around me when I was with Faith. I don't believe she liked her very much. I could understand, after she pulled that thing with Larry.

I painfully remember one day, Trudy and I were walking away from school. A small group of boys followed us. I heard one of them say, "Hey girl, you hear me, you sure do have some fine legs, all smooth and pretty." I turned around to see who was talking, and was immediately scorned with the words, "Ain't anybody talking to you Sissy. I was talking to Trudy." I continued walking beside her only now with my head down, I was close to tears. I knew he wasn't talking to me. No one ever talked to me in this manner. I just wanted to see who was talking. We reached Trudy's home first, and then I continued to walk to my house.

We also had a friend named Janice, which I met through Trudy. Janice was short and quite stunning for her tomboyish ways. Although she kept herself dressed in boyish clothes, the boys still talked to her. When Trudy, Janice and I hung together, I felt pretty; like I belonged. I was so naïve, it never donned on me that there was more to Trudy and Janice's friendship than what I was use to witnessing. I never heard of girls liking girls for more than friendship until Janice and Trudy entered my life. Janice was so in love with Trudy. I discovered this one day when Janice and I were in the hallway of Trudy's house waiting for her.

We were waiting for her to come home. Janice was in such a down mood, I asked her, "What's wrong?" She looked at me with tears in her eyes, and answered, "I love Trudy so much, but she doesn't love me. All she wants to do is hang around those boys." I said, "Well what's wrong with that, she is pretty, and although they try to talk to her she never goes with any of them."

Janice looked at me with those tear filled eyes in amazement. She said, "You don't have the foggiest idea of what I'm saying, do you?" I returned, "What do you mean? Janice what are you talking about?" I retorted. She lowered her head, softly saying. "Trudy and I are together in the same way a boy and girl get together. You know boyfriend or girlfriend? She cares for me but doesn't want anyone to know about us, which is why you have to promise never to tell anyone."

I was stunned, and I didn't know what to say. It also kind of scared me. I was still trying to understand what boys and girls do together. I still didn't know about Pat's mother at this time. Janice tried to explain, "I'm gay. You know, I like girls." "Trudy isn't, but she lets me love her. I'm just never enough for her. She likes the attention the boys give her. I don't know what to do; I love her so much…"

I felt sorry for her. I didn't know what a girl could possibly do for another girl sexually, but I could see it was tearing Janice apart to see Trudy with other people, especially boys. "Why don't you just forget about her, leave her, and find someone else to love you?" I calmly told her. "Look who's talking." I heard myself saying. Like I knew anything about relationships; I still couldn't look Larry in the eye, and I couldn't even tell Carlton I liked him more than as just a friend.

But I thought Janice needed to hear something. "That doesn't work." She said, "I can't give her up; I don't want to live without her. No matter how much she hurts me, it is all better when she comes to me, giving me her attention. I could never give her up." I told her I had to go home, and I left Janice sitting on the porch, waiting for Trudy to come home.

Youth Gone, Love Lost

One day I found myself alone outside of the school building, waiting for lunch time to end, or one of my friends to show up. I saw a group of boys standing near the school doors. They were laughing, and talking loudly about nothing important. One of the boys, a tall good looking man walked over to me. I say he was a man because it was apparent that he was older than the other guys he was with; he actually had a mustache, and a goatee. As he approached me, I could see that he had a beautiful smile, and his eyes smiled along with his mouth. Let's call a spade a spade; he was fine, with a capital F. He asked me for my name, and I told him. He asked me if I went with anyone in the school. I told him no. He said with that smile, "A pretty girl like you don't have a boyfriend? That doesn't seem right." It didn't feel like he was making fun of me, so I didn't take offense.

He continued, "What are you doing tonight around midnight?" I couldn't tell you why I really wanted him to be serious about talking to me, but I also didn't know what to say to him. I decided to just be flippant so I said, "Sleeping." He said, "Well just sleep by the phone tonight. I'm going to call you; answer the phone." I retorted, "What makes you think I'm going to sit by a phone at midnight just to talk to you? I don't even know you. Why do you have to call so late any way, and besides you don't have my phone number." I said this part of the conversation half heartedly. Part of me actually wanted him to be serious, and the other part was afraid he was serious. He laughed, "I have to work, which is why I have to call so late. Don't worry about how I have your phone number. I will call you, and you will answer the phone. Talk to you later, Sissy." Away he went with his buddies, all laughing, and having fun. I knew they couldn't possibly know what Kevin and I had been talking about, but I wondered if the laughter was about me. I felt he had a lot of nerve to expect me to wait for his call, but I kind of liked it.

Sure enough, at midnight I was lying on the couch in our living room, since that was the only phone in the house. I was listening to "Strangers in the Night,[19]" by Frank Sinatra, his "Song of the Year." I waited until I fell asleep. The next morning I got up, and got dressed for school. This went on for three nights. I really wanted him to call me. His demeanor excited me, but he never called. One day, a couple of weeks later, I ran into him again in the school yard. This time when he approached me I was determined that he would not know that I had stayed up for three nights waiting for his call. He immediately took the offense by asking me, "Why didn't you answer the phone when I called?" He had a lot of nerve coming at me like this. He knew damn well he did not call me. But to let him know that, I would have to admit to him that I waited up for his calls. I said, "I don't have time to stay up, and wait for a midnight call, I have to go to school in the morning." I said this because I knew how tired I had been the several days after I had waited. He laughed, and said, "Okay, come walk with me."

We walked around the school grounds, and talked about so many things. He said he would like to see me again. I told him he could see me on the weekend, at 1:00 PM on the playground, up the street from where I lived. He said he would. I didn't want him to come to my house for several reasons. These were the same reasons I always went to my girlfriend's houses rather than let them come to mine. I had eight brothers, and three sisters. Monica had already left home, and she was the only one that tried to keep the house clean. Now it was a shambles. Mom was a good mother, but when it came to cleaning a house, that wasn't her greatest talent. Having eight sons and four daughters didn't help her cleaning skills; she hadn't taught us to clean it up, either, or even think it was a priority. She mostly would lie on the couch, and watched soap operas all day. My two older sisters lived with us but they were never home.

When they were home they only made fun of me, so I definitely didn't want him to meet them. Daddy had promised if he ever got home from work to find a white boy; any boy, is how I interpreted it, on his porch he would hurt him. I could only imagine what he would do to Kevin, him being older, and all. This was so confusing, not only because my father never laid a hand on me, but how ignorant I was in regard to prejudice. These are the only reasons I never took a male, or female for that matter, to my parents' home; not with their knowledge, anyway. Eye witnessing my father's anger made me realize why my mother did all the punishing in the house. I never took anyone else to my house again.

I attended a high school that was two-thirds white. This was due to the recent mandatory busing that was outlined by the government. We lived on the side of the street that was designated to go to this all white high school. Since my sisters, Betsy and Paula were already in high school at the time of the transition, they didn't have to go to the same one that I did. It was during the summer vacation, one Saturday that I went to the playground, specifically to see Kevin who was there, playing basketball with a group of guys.

Although it was disappointing that he was doing something that didn't include me, I felt good watching him, knowing that when the game was over we would talk. I had brought Lawanda and Debra with me. We were sitting on the ground watching the game, when a girl we didn't know walked up to us, and started talking. She introduced herself as Ashley. She was nice enough, and fun to be around. We all sat around watching the guys playing basketball.

Before the game was over, Ashley pulled out a pack of cigarettes, and lit one. She asked us if we wanted one. We all said no. She said, "Do you guys even smoke?" We all said of course we did, we just didn't want one now. For some reason we wanted her to feel that we were more mature than our age. She said, "I bet you don't even know how to smoke. I dare you to inhale." Lawanda said, "I have nothing to prove to you." She walked away with her cousin Debra. They didn't live far from the playground.

Ashley looked at me, with a smirk on her face, "Well." I thought about leaving also because I also didn't smoke. I couldn't leave, Kevin was still playing basketball. I didn't want to look like a kid. I took the cigarette from her, and pulled the smoke into my mouth. I then let it out, saying, "See I told you I smoked." I was hoping this would put an end to this conversation. Ashley wasn't satisfied with my performance. She took the cigarette back, and said, "No, like this." She demonstrated, "Pull the smokes into your lungs slowly; say something, than let it go." I took it back, and did as she did; only this time I choked, and coughed, and I thought I was going to lose whatever was in my stomach.

Ashley laughed so loud everyone in the immediate area, including Kevin, heard it, and saw me in distress. She walked away laughing to herself. This was the first time I really smoked a cigarette. After Kevin's basketball game, and my experience with the first time I really inhaled a cigarette; Kevin came over to talk with me. We made small talk at first but then he asked me if I would go with him to his friend's house up the street. I said I would, but I was really scared. We walked around the corner to his friend's house. I said hello to his friends, but Kevin went right pass him to the upstairs bedroom. This was where he kissed me for the first time. Little did we realize I would never forget this day or him; he gave me my first kiss. I melted into his arms, wanting nothing more than to be in his arms forever. He touched me on my neck, cupping my face, than moving his hands down to my legs, as we fell backward onto the bed. I didn't know what was happening to me, but whatever it was; I wanted it to continue for the rest of my life.

Just when I thought I would explode, Kevin stopped kissing me, sat up, and pulled me up with him. He said we had to go. I didn't understand. I really thought he was going to take me all the way. He just pulled himself together, and when I also was completely dressed, he led me out of the bedroom, and down the stairs. As we got to the front door, he asked if he could see me again. I was so confused by this time; I didn't know what to think. I just knew that I wanted to be with him again. I agreed to see him again if he called me. I left his friends house, confused, and yet excited. I felt that at last I had a boyfriend, someone that cared for me. Kevin called on me several times that month, but it always ended the same way.

The Early Years of Confusion; 1968

In 1968, the *"Year of Revolution[20]"* as many called it; *"Martin Luther King Junior[21]"* was murdered in the month of April, in March of that year, *"Eugene McCarthy[22]"* came within two hundred and thirty votes of unseating the sitting president, *"Lyndon Johnson;[23]"* Johnson said he would not seek re-election, *"Robert Kennedy[24]"* announced that he would be entering the 1968 Presidential Race only to suffer the same fate as Martin Luther King Junior, and for the first time in my sixteen years went to another state.

This was a year that I will never forget. I wanted to go to Georgia with my Aunt, but my mother told her sister that if she took me I would get everybody killed. My mother continued to say that I had no control over my mouth. I never did understand why she said that since I rarely said anything to anyone; I guess that was just her opinion. Later, I was told by my aunt that she was successful in changing my mother's mind. The day we left, it happened to be the day Martin Luther King was killed, and all hell broke loss in America.

I remember the highway was full of police, and sheriff vehicles. On the radio we could hear the news broadcast saying that someone was killed and the country was full of riots everywhere. The police pulled over my uncle's car, and I was told to lie down in the back seat. I remember being so scared. They didn't find whatever they were looking for so they just confiscated my uncle's six pack of beer. I didn't know anything about Martin Luther King or whatever the racial tension was all about. We arrive in Atlanta with no other problems.

One day, after I returned to Milwaukee, I was baby-sitting for a friend's aunt. My friend may have had a life, but I rarely had something to do. This is why I was usually available to babysit. Their house was located in the neighborhood I lived in. I enjoyed babysitting because it was a time when I didn't have to be around my family, I could play my music, and I could pretend the child was mine. I called my friend Johnny over to listen to music while I baby sat. Johnny was about the same age as me. One of Johnny's legs was shorter than the other. Some of our classmates would make fun of him, but he was a good friend to me. While we were listening to music, Johnny asked me if I was seeing anyone in particular. I told him I was seeing Kevin Johns. He laughed, and asked me, "Don't you know he goes with Theresa Sheppard?" I told him I didn't believe him. He said, "Ask anyone, he's taking her to the prom." I didn't want to hear this. I wished I hadn't heard it, but it kept ringing in my ears. I told Johnny, "I thought you were my friend, but instead you are cruel, and I need you to leave." After he left I sat on the couch, and cried. I told myself, this couldn't be true, but deep down I knew it was. I loved Kevin so much.

The following day Kevin came by my house to see me. I stood on the front porch, and asked him, "What do you want?" He said, "What's the matter with you?" I said, "I just found out you're going out with Theresa, and you're taking her to the prom." He said, "So what? What does that have to do with us?" I looked at him in disbelief. I couldn't believe he was actually admitting that he was seeing her; much less acting like it shouldn't make a difference. I said, "Kevin, I care a lot for you, but you want your cake, and you want to eat it too. If you're seeing both of us, you must be using one of us.

Since you're taking her to the prom, I'm afraid it must be me." He reached out for me but I backed up. He said, "Your logic doesn't make sense. If I'm using you, what am I using you for? What have I taken from you? Sex, money, what? Have I even asked you for anything? I just enjoy being around you." I thought about what he was saying, I felt foolish, and hurt by the new information, I wished I hadn't heard. I also felt he was trivializing the situation; I wanted to rethink my logic and consider whether he might be right. I retorted, "You asked me for seven cents and I want it back, now." He was laughing by now. I continued, "You might think this is funny but I don't. I am not going to see you, as long as you're with her. Since you are going to the prom with her, I don't feel right about having her return all the formal attire, so goodbye."

I knew that there was no chance for me to acquire clothes for the prom. I knew my parents couldn't or wouldn't even consider the expense. This made me remember just how poor we really were. It was not only that I couldn't afford to go; my parents would never allow me to go, since I was only six-teen, and Kevin was nineteen. I didn't feel it was right for two women; such as I felt I was, to go with the same man. I also wanted him to be more than just a friend. I turned around, and walked swiftly into the house, without another word from him.

I knew Theresa. She was in my chemistry class. One Monday, after the prom, I went up to her, and asked, "Do you know Kevin Johns?" She said, "Yes, I use to go with him, but we broke up, why?" I told her I liked him, and I just wanted to know if she would mind if I started seeing him again. She said, "I'm through with him, if you want him that's fine with me. I don't want him."

I was happy, since this meant I could go out with him again. That evening I called him, and told him what she had said. He said, "I told you that, now what?" I told him we could continue seeing each other. I continued to see him every chance I could. One day I was on the bus, going to a football game, when a group of girls on the bus started talking loud about Theresa, and me going out with the same guy. I walked over, and sat close to Theresa to ask her was it true that she was seeing Kevin again. She said yes it was true. In my naivety I said, "But I asked you, and you said you were through with him, and didn't want him anymore." She only smiled, and said, "I know, but we made up." I was devastated that Kevin hadn't told me.

When I saw Kevin again, I had to tell him what happened. He said, "I am so tired of people talking about our situation. You tell me, what do you want to do about it? Yes, I'm seeing Theresa and yes I'm seeing you. I'm sleeping with Theresa but I'm not doing anything with you because I want to marry you. You're a good girl my sweet lady and I want to keep you that way." As usual Kevin said just what I wanted to hear. But it still bothered me that he was still seeing Theresa, and sleeping with her was just too unbearable to believe. But whatever he wanted, I was willing to do, just to keep him in my arms. So when I saw Theresa, and her friends at school, I ignored them. When I was with Kevin, he made me feel like I was the only one. I was never to tell anyone that we were still together. I understood this was in order to keep the peace, not just with the public, but for my own peace of mind. I held in my heart the knowledge that Kevin still loved me, and his wanting to marry me, meant so much to me. I would remember what he said, and tell myself that Theresa was just a whore that he used to satisfy his male cravings.

All of his buddies knew about us, and I thought that was enough. Although to keep up the cool façade wasn't easy. I knew that it hurt me down to my toes but what else could I do, I loved him. From day to day, especially when I saw Theresa, I would remember this girl was in my man's arms. It seemed that Kevin and I kept having squabbles about Theresa, and our relationship, so one day he said, "Let's just call it quits." I didn't know what to do. I loved Kevin. I couldn't talk him out of his decision. As the days passed, I craved for his touch, and thought of nothing but his voice in my ear, telling me how much he really cared for me. Kevin and I had a mutual friend named Gerald. Although Gerald was Kevin's best friend first, I enjoyed talking to him, so I was his friend also. I usually felt close to Kevin when I was with Gerald. I always hoped inside that Kevin would show up, when I was with him. Gerald was dark skinned, overweight, and short. Gerald's mother worked at a distillery. She would bring home large bottles of vodka, and Gerald was allowed to drink all he wanted.

I was seventeen, and I had never drunk anything alcoholic before. One day, I had just gotten in another argument with Kevin, I asked Gerald to bring me something to drink. I wanted to get drunk, not knowing what drunk was. He was at my door within an hour. We stood in the hallway between the outer, and the inside door, talking. He told me, "Now all I have is this amount." It was an eight ounce glass of vodka. He continued, "If you really want to get drunk, you're going to have to drink it all up, real fast. Drink it all at once." I, being new at drinking, believed him. I took the glass, and held it to my lips. It smelled terrible. I started to chicken out, but remembered that I had never drank before, and decided I wanted to know how it felt. I turned the glass up, and drank it all at the same time as Gerald had instructed.

He left after that. I didn't want my mother to see me drunk, so I went upstairs to my room. Within the next few minutes I felt the room spinning, and I couldn't control my body. I ran to the bathroom, and started throwing up my insides. I felt as though I would never stop. Finally when I felt it had stopped, I ran downstairs to tell my mother I was sick. I felt like dying. She took one look at me, and smelled the vodka. She then said, "You're drunk! You've been drinking. Get out of my sight; you're on your own." I dragged myself back upstairs, and continued to make trips to the bathroom in between lying on the spinning bed. I thought I was going to die. For the next five years, if I so much as smelled vodka, it seemed I would get sick. Although I did a lot of drinking in my life, I never drank vodka again. I was eight-teen before I forgave Gerald for his prank.

Girls Just Want to Have Fun

I would go to Gerald's basement apartment because we always had a good time there; listening to music, and talking about our other friends. It was during one of these get-togethers when it dawned on me how to get rid of Theresa. Since all Kevin really wanted from her was sex with her, why don't I have sex with him. The problem was my virginity, and Kevin made it quite clear that he liked it that way. He was not about to change it. Gerald was drinking vodka, as usual, that he got from his mother. He was feeling pretty good, and I knew it wouldn't be long before he passed out.

I sat on the couch next to him, and asked him, "Gerald, if you would help me get Kevin for myself, I would be so grateful; there isn't much I wouldn't do to pay you back." He said, "Sissy you know you wouldn't have to pay me back, I'm crazy about you, I know how much you love Kevin, and he is my best friend. I never did like Theresa. I think you would be a much better girlfriend so I would do anything I can to help you, but I can't think of anything I can do to help. "I know that Kevin is going to Theresa for sex. Now if I could give him sex, he wouldn't need her anymore." Gerald seemed to be following my plan along with the conversation, but the light bulb still hadn't come on, "Okay but what has that got to do with me.

Where do I come in?" I got closer to him, and said, "I have a plan. If you take my virginity, Kevin won't have any more reason to see her. I'm the only woman he needs." Gerald looked up at me in shock, "You have got to be kidding. Have you lost your mind? Kevin would kill me." I looked at him with tears in my eyes, "Yes I've thought about this a lot,

23

but I don't have any choice. Kevin won't take it, and all my virginity is doing is standing between us. Please Gerald, I'm desperate." It seemed that Gerald was too afraid of what Kevin might do if he had sex with me. I sipped on my drink while Gerald drank two of three more. When the time seemed right, I made my move.

I touched him between his legs through his pants. I kept telling him that it would be alright. No one was going to know but him and me. Finally Gerald climbed on top of me. He smelled of cigarettes and gin. He was heavy, since he was twice the size he should be for his age. I kept reminding myself "This is necessary in order to get Kevin to love me, and only with me." As Gerald took off his pants, and straddled me I looked up at the ceiling which was covered in ceiling tiles. While Gerald took my virginity I lay there counting the holes in the ceiling.

When he finished he rolled off, and went to sleep. Once I pulled myself together, I walked home. I was so proud of myself. I had finally done something to get him back. He wouldn't have any other reasons not to leave Theresa. When I got home, I immediately called Kevin, and when he answered the phone I said, "Hello Kevin, what are you doing?" He said, "Why are you calling me at this time of night? You know my grandmother is sleep, and might get mad." "I know but I have something important to tell you." He hesitated to answer, "What is that?" "I'm not a virgin any more I had sex. You don't need to be with Theresa. You don't need to quit me?" He sounded quite upset, "You did what? You're not what.... Who?" "It's not important who; all you have to know is that it's over, I'm seven-teen, and no longer a virgin. Now we can be together." He kept repeating the same question, "Who?" I finally told him "It was Gerald." I added; "...but he really didn't want to, I asked him to do it, and he was drunk. You know how much I love you, but you wouldn't do it, and you keep seeing Theresa. I needed to do something so there wouldn't be anything between us."

Kevin seemed quite upset as he spoke, "First of all, out of all the people you could have done it with, why did you pick my best friend? Second, that is the stupidest thing I have ever heard. Where are you at now?" "I'm at home. Why?" It didn't seem like he had any emotions, in his voice, except anger. He said, "I want you to get over here right now." I was beginning to get scared by the tone of his voice, "Why? What about your grandmother?" "Don't worry about that. Let me worry about that, you just get over here, now." He sounded like he was very upset. He hung up the phone. It was after ten o'clock at night, and I didn't know what he wanted, but all I wanted was to have him in my life again. I loved him so much. I didn't worry about what my parents would do to me if they caught me sneaking out at this time of night. It didn't take me long to arrive at his house. He opened the door before I could knock. We quietly walked up the stairs to his bedroom.

Once there, he didn't say a word. He just took me in his arms, and started caressing me. As usual, I felt the warmth coming from my loins up my spine, all the way up to my head. I didn't want it to ever stop. His hands were on my blouse, taking time not to rush me. He touched me with the hands of a skilled lover. He reached down, and removed my skirt, so softly I didn't even notice it was gone. He laid me back onto the bed; he removed my panties, and massaged me between my legs. I was about to lose my mind when this time he didn't stop. He lowered his body onto mine, and I felt his manhood enter me. It was so hot, yet soothing. It was like the dam to my love had finally burst. This was not what I felt with Gerald. I loved Kevin even more than I did before this. I knew I would do anything this man asked me. When it was over, he lay back, and lit a cigarette. We shared it.

Then he finally said, "Why did you fuck Gerald?" I reminded him, "I told you why. I love you so, but you wouldn't do it. I felt as if you weren't taking me or my love for you seriously. I believed my virginity is why you didn't want me." He softly touched my face, "Sex is not why I broke it off with you. I stopped seeing you because I felt I was hurting you more by being with you. I never stopped caring for you." It was then that I realized that Kevin had never said he loved me. It was always me saying "I love you," but he never did. I thought about this, but decided I didn't care. I would love him so much he would fall in love with me. Just being with him was enough. My life became very dependent on his phone calls. He would call me, and say nothing more than, "Come over here." I would run to him as fast as I could. He would make love to me then I would leave.

One day I asked him, "Kevin, does your grandmother know I'm up here?" He said, "Yes." I said, "What does she think we're doing up here? Isn't she worried?" He smiled at me, and said, "She thinks I know what I'm doing." I asked, "Do you?" He said with laughter in his voice, "I hope I do." My life for the next year depended on Kevin's mood. What he wanted. What he thought, I thought. I had no self esteem, all I knew was that my happiness depended on whether he wanted to see me or not. It never dawned on me that we never used a condom. Never even a thought about it. One day I voiced my concerns to him...

"Kevin, I'm afraid you don't love me as much as I love you. Sometimes I feel you don't love me at all. You're just using me for sex. Is this true?" Kevin who was lying on the bed, with me in his arms answered, "Sissy, no matter what I say, you would feel the way you do. If I told you I loved you, would it change how you felt about me? Why is it so important that I say what you want to hear? Isn't it more important how I treat you? How you feel when you're with me? I can't change your mind about how you think, but I can do something about helping you to be happy again.

I don't think we should see each other again. I feel it hurts you too much to stay in this relationship and I can't commit to you as much as you want me to." I was shocked at how cold he could be. Would he really just stop seeing me? Just for asking a question. I felt the panic raise up in my throat. "Kevin, you can't mean, you can't be serious. I'm sorry, it is okay, and I won't ask any more questions. I really need to be with you. Please don't do this?" "No I really think this is what needs to happen.

The last thing I want to do is hurt you. This relationship hurts you more than anything, so this is the last time you will come here. Let's get up, and get dressed so you can go." I dressed in silence. I knew when Kevin made up his mind on something, he meant it. I didn't know how I would survive without him, but I had to try. Two weeks went by. I would stare at the phone when I was home, hoping he would call. I would search the crowd of people outside of my school, hoping to see him. But he was never there. I felt so alone.

Night Club Life; 1969

It was the end of 1969 when I listened to my favorite singer; *"Diana Ross.*[25]*"* There were many important events; such as, when the *"Viet Cong and North Vietnamese*[26]*"* suddenly launched their strongest offensive. One Saturday, I was walking down the street, when I heard a familiar voice behind me. It was my friend Freddy in a car with about three other men. He asked me if I wanted a ride home. I was bored, so I agreed, and got into the car. Instead of driving me toward my house they drove toward the lake. I objected but they weren't listening, they were laughing like they knew something I didn't. When we got to the lake, they all got out of the car. I was afraid but I got out too. I pleaded with them to take me home. They laughed, and said the only way they would take me home was if I had sex with them; all of them.

I cried, and again pleaded with them, "Take me home. I thought you guys were my friends." Again they laughed, "The only thing I want to be friendly with is between your legs." I wasn't even sure which one said this. Now I got mad, "If you don't take me home immediately, I will start walking, and call the police when I get home." They thought that was so funny. Freddy said, "Go ahead, and call the police, I'm leaving Milwaukee, because I've joined the army. You're the one that got into the car, and you don't know any of the other's names." I hesitated, because he was right. This was my fault.

I turned, and started to walk away from them. They didn't try to stop me, instead they just kept laughing. I walked until I couldn't see them anymore. I didn't know where I was going or what I was going to do. I stayed quite a distance from the lake. I wasn't even sure how to get home, what direction to take. After walking for a long time, I decided to stop at a house to ask for help. I was on the white side of town. Beautiful houses in the neighborhood. When I knocked on a door, a woman answered.

She seemed very nice. Her smile was warm, and compassionate. She gave me a drink of brandy to calm me down. I don't know if she knew or even cared that I wasn't twenty-one. She heard my tale, and said, "Don't you worry, child. I'll just have my husband take you home." I was so grateful to her; tears again came to my eyes. I followed him to the garage, and got into his car. He drove toward my home. Before we even left the neighborhood, he started talking about sex, "You're a very pretty girl for a black girl. I know you've got many boyfriends. I know how grateful you say you are, but I want to know how grateful you really are." He said, as I just wondered how far he would take me before he put me out for not being grateful enough. "You know it's not as if you haven't put out before, I just feel that you should have sex with me. I, of course, will pay you. It's not like the four boys. It is just you and I, and you'd get some money to buy whatever you like afterwards."

Again I started to panic. I started crying again, "I'm not like that. I never had sex before. Mister, please take me home." I guess my tears, and the lie I told got through to him. I was not about to have sex with this old, fat, white man, who felt he could just through money at me, and I would sell my respect. He must have believed me because he didn't say anything anymore. He just continued to drive, and when he got a block away from where I lived, I asked him to let me out. I didn't want this dirty old man to see where I lived. Once I got into the house I went immediately to the phone, and called Kevin. I told him of my ordeal, and he seemed compassionate enough. He did want to know, "Why in hell did you get into the car to begin with?" I tried to explain, "I thought Freddy was a nice person, and I really didn't think he would do something like this to me." Kevin said, "Okay, so it's over now. You have got to be more careful about who you trust."

I was quietly crying into the phone when I said, "Kevin, this is your fault too, if you hadn't broke up with me I wouldn't have been so bored, and gotten into the car. I miss you so much. Please can I see you tonight, just one more time?" He was quiet for a moment, "If you come here you will hate yourself again. You know I can't give you what you need. I'm just what you don't need tonight. I can only give you what I have to offer, no more." "I know that Kevin, I swear I will never question your feelings again. I will do whatever you say, without question. Please? I understand that you can't give me what I need, so just give me what I want than. I need to be with you." Kevin was quiet for a long time while I held my breath. I knew he was deep in thought.

He finally said, "Okay, come on over, but don't ever question my feeling for you again. I can only feel so much, and I can't be anyone else. I won't be responsible for your feelings. Do you understand?" "Yes, I understand, I promise I will bite my lip. I will not question you again. I'll be right over." This is how our relationship went for another six months. I loved him so, I kept telling myself, "Okay. I can live with his rules more than I can live without him."

As time went on, I no longer lived just to see Kevin. Don't get me wrong, I still loved him, but I couldn't just sit at home, and hope he would call me. After all, I was eight-teen. I would hang around a neighborhood pool hall around the corner from my house. All the people that knew Kevin would congregate there. Sometimes he would even arrive there. He never acted like he was with me, but sometimes when he left; I would meet him outside, and would go home with him. I even heard he was now going with a girl named Nona Boggs. We never discussed her, because I had made the promise that I wouldn't ask questions.

Sometimes I would see her in the neighborhood. She didn't know about Kevin and me, so I decided to make friends with her. I would listen to her talk about Kevin, and how much she loved him. I never told her about us because he had told me not to question him. He didn't come out, and say it again, but it was understood. Several times Kevin would come by her house when I was there.

There was a definite chill in the air when all three of us were together. Kevin and I just acted like we didn't like each other, thus explaining the tension between us to Nona. I would excuse myself, so they could be alone. I would leave knowing he was with her. I couldn't have that, could I? I would go next door to Paul's house, and call over to her house. She would always tell Kevin that I was on the phone. She felt that since I was her best friend, and he was her man, she wanted us to get along.

She would plead with me to talk to Kevin. "You two shouldn't be like that. Just say hello, okay?" She wanted me to be nice to Kevin. I could do that. He would get on the phone, and I would immediately say something like, "I'm next door at Paul's house. I'm all hot, and bothered. I need you in me baby, so I know you can't answer me right now, so I will wait thirty minutes. If you're not here, I'm going home. You're decision is simple, goody, goody or me, choose, see you." I would hang up knowing he would choose me every time." It would make me feel powerful to get him to leave "Miss goody two shoes." as I called her. It was probably because she now had Kevin in the way I use too. He was no longer saving me for marriage. He would act like he was making small talk with me on the phone. He would then give the phone back to Nona. I don't know what he would tell her but within the half hour he would always be in my arms. This is how my summer was spent. Whatever life I valued was centered on days or hours I was able to be with Kevin. It wasn't just about sex with us, I could listen to him talk for hours.

There were other situations that arose that didn't include Kevin; although they didn't seem really important to me, these things only occurred because Kevin didn't have time for me. I had to continue on with my life without him so I spent a lot of time outside of my home. After Janice's confession, we became good friends. Janice was interested in music. She played the drums. She was a member of a very good band which was made up of a singer named Howard, and his male family members. She wasn't related to them but she was a very talented drummer. I would accompany her to the clubs they were to play at. Most of these places were night clubs. Janice and I were seven-teen at this time, but no one asked us for identification. This was an exciting, and fun time in my life. No one treated us like children. As a matter of fact, they treated us just like adults. The guys in the band never tried to touch us or make advances at us. I soon discovered why.

I was eight-teen when I started to go to the clubs with my sister Paula. She and I would get dressed to kill on the weekends. We always arrived together but Paula would always leave the clubs with some man, or other, leaving me to fend for myself. I would drink until I felt it, then I would walk home, alone. One day, Paula invited me to go to some of her friends' house with her, after the club closed. At least I thought they were Paula's friends, since that is what she told me.

It seemed as if the closer it got to the club's closing time, the weirder I was beginning to feel. By the time we left the club everything was spinning, and I was feeling ill. I don't think I was even standing or walking on my own feet when we left the club. When we arrived at the house I don't remember going upstairs with a man, but I do remember waking up with him inside of me. He was rough, and he hurt me. I tried to push him off me, but he was too strong. All I could do was pray for him to finish what he was doing so I could get away. It seemed like it lasted forever.

After he finished dumping in me, he got up, and asked me if I was alright. I don't know how I knew it, but I felt that I was in danger, and had to make him think I cared about him also. I kissed him, and told him he was the greatest. He helped me up off the mat on the floor, where he had just finished raping me. Whatever it was that he had drugged me with seem to be dissipating, and I could see clear enough to walk down the stairs myself. He walked me to the door. I didn't know where my sister was but I heard her voice in the background. "Sissy, get out of here. Get out while you can."

My head was still spinning. He opened the door, and told me he would see me later. I started walking home. I didn't know where I was or how I found the strength to keep walking. I took each step, looking around at a world that kept spinning around in my head. I don't know how I got home but once I got there, I went to my room, and passed out. I woke up the next day, wondering what had happened, and where was Paula. I didn't know what to do. Should I tell my mother? Would Paula want me to tell mom what we were doing to get into this mess? The questions rang in my ear, over, and over again. Instead of telling someone about the night before, I told no one.

Three days later, Paula showed up back at home. She screamed at me, "Why didn't you help me? They had me there all this time, selling me over, and over to who ever had ten dollars. How could you leave me there like that? You never think of anyone but yourself. I told them to let you go, and I would stay with them, but I thought sure you would have sense enough to send help."

All I could say was, "I didn't know what to do. I never imagined you were in trouble. You said they were your friends. I thought you wanted to be there with them. I was mad at you for letting that bastard rape me. Paula I swear I didn't know what was happening. I thought they were your friends. Besides, I wouldn't know which house we were at anyway. I couldn't even remember what street we were on, or how I found my way home. I didn't know." I don't think she ever forgave me for not getting her some help. We never spoke of the situation again.

We All Have to Grow Up

One night everyone except Janice and I had left to go out to a night club. We had the whole place to ourselves. Janice, I could tell, was in a weird mood. She asked me, "Sissy, have you ever made love with anyone?" I told her I had not. She asked, "Not even a boy?" Again I shook my head. I have no idea why I was lying, especially after she had been so candid with me. I was feeling nervous about where this conversation was going. She continued, "I've been looking at you lately, and you are a very pretty girl. Why haven't you had any boyfriends?" I did have a boyfriend, his name was Kevin Johns, but I didn't feel she had a need to know. I had been lying for so long it came naturally. I just said, "I don't know." Janice came closer to me at this time; she put her hand on my arm, caressing it ever so softly. She said, "Sissy, I am very attracted to you. Would you consider being with me?"

I knew what she was talking about, but this whole conversation was beginning to unnerve me. As a matter of fact this whole situation alarmed me. I began to feel my face getting warm, my stomach had butterflies, and my legs felt weak. I said, "What do you mean, be with you? I'm already with you. You're the closest friend I have. I care for you also." Janice stopped rubbing my arm. Instead she walked over to where the group kept the liquor. She poured two drinks, gave me one then said, "Here have a sip. It will relax you." I seldom drank, but at this moment Janice was making me very nervous. I took the drink. I didn't sip it. I started to drink the whole glass, but I had learned my lesson by Gordy's prank. Janice then said, "Now isn't that better? Sissy, I know we're friends, but do you remember me telling you about Trudy?" I said,

33

"Yes." She continued, "We broke up; I thought I loved her so much, but it was a painful love. Love shouldn't hurt so badly."

Damn, I thought to myself, I should be writing her words. I knew all about painful love. She continued, "Since I've met you, I've developed strong feelings for you, like I had for Trudy. Won't you even consider trying what I have to offer? If you don't like it, we'll forget all about it. We will always be friends; I just want to love you." I really felt uncomfortable, and wanted to leave. I didn't want her to feel for me like she had liked Trudy. I didn't want her to see me act like a child either, but all I wanted now was my mother. I was beginning to wonder where and when the other guys were coming back. She again approached me, ever so slowly. She touched my face, and looked deep into my eyes. When Janice spoke again she said, "I know you like me too, and you're curious about the world I can give you. Don't stop me. Just let it happen, you won't regret it." She lowered her lips unto mine, they were so soft, and she smelled so good. When she touched me, it sent shock waves through my body. She made an attempt to unbutton my blouse, and it was at this time that I realized that the guys were not going to miraculously come home to save me. The emotions I felt at this time were so overwhelming I didn't want her to stop. I felt myself drift along as if I were someone else, standing outside of my body.

All I could think of was how I could get out of this situation without jeopardizing my standing with the group. If I allowed her to continue, would she tell them? If so would they feel as I did, would they say, "Oh, that's nasty, and so are you." Then they would surely put me out of the group. If I didn't let this happen, would she tell them? If so, would they be on her side, and put me out of the group because they felt I was too immature to continue with the group. I finally decided that this was not for me.

I enjoyed my friendship with Janice, the close relationship with the group, and going out to adult nightclubs until wee hours of the night. I pushed her away, and told her, "I realize that you are living in a different world than what I am use to, but you have to understand that our friendship depends on your understanding of how I feel. I am not gay. I understand how you felt about Trudy, but coming at me would put you back in the same boat she left you in. I don't love you that way. I enjoy being with you but if you can't be my best friend because of the emotions you feel, I'm sorry. I enjoy going out with the band but the price is too high." I went to the door, and looked back to see how she was reacting to my statement. I walked home alone. I have no idea of what she told them when they returned, but they were her friends before I met them so she could keep them.

I didn't see any point continuing my relationship with any of them. I stopped going to the practice sessions with the band. My relationship with the guys in the band was never the same. I stopped attending anything that included Janice. This was my first experience with a woman, and I knew I would never forget it. Up until this, Janice and I had a great relationship. I guess it alarmed me, to be in a relationship with a girl.

Street Smarts for Survival; 1969

I was eight-teen, it was 1969, and I could see the headlines as the tickertape rolled by. There were so many historical events happening during this year. Such as when *"Richard Milhous Nixon[27]"* succeeded Lyndon Baines Johnson as the thirty seventh president of the United States, *"James Earl Ray[28]"* pleaded guilty to assassinating Martin Luther King Jr. Although he later retracted his guilty plea, the *"Apollo 10[29]"* returned to earth, *"Judy Garland[30]"* died of a drug overdose, members of a cult; led by *"Charles Manson,[31]"* murdered *"Sharon Tate;[32]"* she was eight months pregnant. A miracle; *"New York Mets[33]"* won the World Series, *"Sesame Street[34]"* premiered on the National Educational Television (NET) network, the *"Black Panther Party[35]"* members; Fred Hampton and Mark Clark are dead; shot in their sleep during a riot by *"four-teen Chicago police officers,[36]"* reports are linking first strain of the *"AIDS virus[37]"* (HIV) migrated to the U.S. via Haiti, *"Dwight D. Eisenhower,[38]"* thirty-fourth President of the U.S. died, and *Sissy B. Smith* was emancipated from her childhood home.

After the previous incident I stopped going to clubs with Paula, I never trusted her again. We would get dressed, go out to play cards and get drunk although not together. I was still in high school, and it was a fun life, but it wasn't anything to continue to do for the rest of my life. Well at this point in my life, it seemed like it was all a dream, or a nightmare depending on who is living it. One day I was just a girl that loved to play with her dolls, than I found myself drugged, raped and taken for granted by the man I loved. It was really confusing since

I loved Paula, she was my sister, but I blamed her for getting me in the rape situation. I never saw the bastards that were with us that day.

If I did, I didn't recognize them. Sometimes it seemed like a dream, but it mostly seemed like a nightmare. Up until this incident, I usually went out alone; of which I never had a negative event happen. I never really hung out with Paula, so since she didn't ask me to go out with her any more, she went on with her life, and I went on with my life. Look what happened when I did try to be with her. Anyway, I still loved Kevin; he continued to have his way with me, and anyone else he wanted to, it was fine with me.

I wasn't trying to get married or anything. I just wanted to have fun so this lifestyle was fine with me. At least this is what I told myself. I went out every night, hanging with the guys. I guess my mother decided she needed to interject some motherly love. I say this because I don't remember momma ever really talking to me mother to daughter about: good advice, concern for my welfare, just talking about nothing; these things never came from my mother's mouth to me.

All I really remember her talking about is "Go wash the dishes," "Go to the store for me," or "Get out of here with that noise." I can't blame her, I loved her. I imagine she did have twelve children. She was either too tired or just didn't have any more conversation in her. One day my mother, for some reason or other was trying to reenter my life. Only now I really wasn't interested in having a mother. An example of her motherly love was demonstrated when I was six-teen years old; I started getting headaches. My mother decided to take me to the doctor's office.

After taking a variety of test it was time to speak with the doctor about what they discovered from the tests. We listened to the doctor as he told us that I suffered from migraine headaches. I remembered how happy I was to be with my mother, alone. I didn't have to share her with any of my siblings. This was the first time I could remember being with her, just she and I. We talked, laughed and just acted silly that whole day. I discovered my mother was really good to talk to and she actually had a great sense of humor. I loved it. When we got home, I cheerfully went to my room. I really enjoyed being with my mother all day. She on the other hand went to my father's room, as soon as we got home to tell him about our outing. They didn't sleep in the same room anymore. He came to my room, and asked in a knowing way…

"So you've been drinking, and you're having hangovers every morning, huh?" I was shocked to hear this, since that was nowhere close to what the doctor said. I asked him, "Daddy, what are you talking about?" He looked at me with his all knowing glare, "Your mother just told me the doctor said there was nothing wrong with you but you're drinking every night."

I had tears in my eyes by now. I felt betrayed by my mother. I felt rejected by my father, and I was confused. I told him, "But Daddy that is not what the doctor told us. He said I had something called migraines." Daddy turned, and walked over to my mother, and said, "You're the biggest liar in the world. Why would you lie on that girl?"

He pushed her out of his way. He put on his hat, and left the house. I didn't know it at the time, but daddy suffered from migraines also. He knew it could be passed on through heredity, and for me to even know the words "migraine headache" was enough proof of what the doctor had said.

After daddy left the house, Mamma came up to me; she was mad. I could tell she was going to beat me with her belt. She said, "How dare you contradict what I said to your father. If I said you were drinking, you were." I said, "But momma, that isn't what the doctor said. I was there. He said my headaches were called migraines." She was really mad now. She walked over to me, and started hitting me with the belt. I was crying, while she kept telling me, "What I say is right, and don't you ever contradict me again. Do you hear me, Missy? Do you understand what I am telling you?"

As I said, I was hurt, and not only from the belt. I couldn't believe this woman was the same woman that had spent the day with me, laughing, playing and bonding. It just didn't make any sense, to me and I couldn't understand how this was such a big deal. Anyway, by now she was worked up, and I was crying, kneeling on the floor. This is when she picked up a large piece of wood. Someone later told me it was called a "two by four."

My mother started to bring the wood upon my head with it when my sisters; Betsy, and Paula, grabbed her hands and took the wood from her, and lead her back to her room. Somehow my mother had changed the roles in this play. She was now the victim, and I was the villain. As she walked away from me mamma looked back at me with hate in her eyes. She screamed at me to stay out of her face. I did just that. I still don't know why this incident was so important or why my mother had turned on me so. Well as I was saying, my mother rarely even noticed me or spoke to me. So when she stopped speaking to me after this incident,

I didn't miss her, I was relieved. I guess because we had a large family, it never struck her that I was around. This worked for me. One day momma came over to me and said, was "You look like you're going out." I guess you could say I was being combatant, but I felt I had to be on guard that day. I said, "I'm going to meet some friends at the corner store." This corner store was actually a pool hall around the corner. I didn't want to let her know it was a place where these groups of kids get together to act grown up. She said, "Well you can go but be back here by twelve o'clock, that's midnight lady." I had just turned eight-teen and she had never given me a curfew before. I just looked at her and said, "Whatever."

I was so upset with her, and I felt she was wrong to tell me what time to come home after all this time. After all, I was now eight-teen now; didn't that make me grown. I felt she just wanted to test me to see if she could still tell me to do what she wanted me to do. I was still in high school, but like I said, I had been going and doing what I wanted since I was six-teen. Hell, I had been going to the night clubs since I was seven-teen. So this night I went to the pool hall, and of course, there was no one there.

I was about to have a life changing event happen to me, and there was no one at the pool hall to tell. There was the man that ran the place, and maybe two other people, playing pool. I sat at a table in the back, reading a comic book. Yes, it was 1969, and my being eight-teen meant something to me, even if no one else cared. I really felt I had a point to make. I sat there until midnight... yet nothing happened to remove my attention from my comic book. That is just how bored I was. When it came time for the pool hall to close, two AM, I got up, and reluctantly walked around the corner knowing I was about to walk into my mother's waiting arms. "Yeah, right!"

When I walked into the house she was standing there, looking at me with determination in her eyes. We both knew what was about to happen. She said the first word, "Go get me a belt." This was not a question. I walked over to where I knew she kept the belt she usually used to beat us with. I handed it to her. She said, "Now you know I'm going to have to beat you... I told you to be here before midnight." "I agreed with you that you had the right to tell me, but I didn't agree to be here." I said, "Momma, you asked me to get the belt, and I did, you tell me you feel you have to beat me, and I can agree with you that you feel you have to. But I can't let you hit me with that belt. You have always told us that there is room for only two grown people in a household. You are one, and daddy is the other. But I feel I am grown, today. So since you feel you have to beat me, and I know I can't let that happen, I realize I have to leave your house at this time. Momma, I love you." With this comment I leaned over, and kissed my mother on her forehead. I turned and walked out of the door.

I didn't know where I was going, anymore than I knew why I had just done what I did. As I walked the streets, I noticed it was dark, lonely and ominous with no one on the streets. I knew I couldn't just keep walking the streets, but I really didn't have a clue what I was supposed to do at this time. I knew that both of my sisters, Betsy, and Paula had left home, but they both came back to receive an ass whipping. I always said to myself that I would never return to that.

It wasn't because of the whipping, as much as it was because of the disrespect I felt the whipping represented. I knew I was grown, and I would not go back to my mother's house. This was not an option. I knew it was time to get my life together on my own. I hadn't thought it out this far. I was too stubborn to go back, and tell my mother how ridiculous I felt. But to tell you the truth, I really wasn't afraid. I don't know if I was too stupid to be or whether I had just spent so much time out in the streets already that even the streets felt like home.

Only the Strong Survive

Finally I thought about what I needed to do. I had an aunt who lived a few blocks away. Of course this was my mother's sister, but it wasn't like we were fighting. I just felt I was too old to get a whipping, or to be told what I should or shouldn't do. I had to get off the streets, right? When I arrived at Aunt Dolores' house, she welcomed me with open arms. She did wonder what I was doing outside this time of the morning, so I told her what had happened. She didn't judge me or take momma's side either. She just took me in, had me change clothes into one of her soft night gowns, and I went to bed in her guest room, it smelled so much better than I had ever slept in before. Once I woke up, the next morning, I realized I couldn't stay there. It was just like staying at my mother's house, and somehow it just didn't seem right. This was what I remembered about my teen years because at this point was where my teen years ended.

I had lots of things on my mind so as I walked the streets or even in my aunt's bed to go to sleep. I felt my ethics were closely related to my value system. The things I valued most were made up of what I believed. What I was brought up to believe, is what I considered right or wrong. What makes a person believe something is important. As I grew older, I saw my parents doing things that they told me not to do. I grew up, and once out into the world I found that people would do whatever is necessary to accomplish the task of survival.

In turn, my value system became manipulated by many things within my environment. This also changed my ethics in such a way that I could tell that whatever I did was going to be okay, for me. My children will also do whatever they deem necessary for their survival one day. As my children grow up; they also will grow older. They will also grow up in their own environment; hearing, seeing, and rationalizing the reasons why. I am at this point in my life where my value system is going to determine the course of the rest of my life. I mention all of this to clarify why I am now taking the directional changes in my life.

When I left my aunt's house, the next morning, I had to rely on the growth of my ethics and my value system which had been taught to me throughout my previous years. I was previously living in my parent's home. Now I was on the streets alone, and I hadn't been brought up to believe in God's grace. So because of this I felt I was alone. I went to the club scene that night. I didn't know where I was going or what I was going to do but I did know that I had to survive. I also knew that I was not going to go back to my mother's house. I truly believed that there were only two grown people in a household; my mom and dad were grown in their home. I also knew that I had gotten to the point in my life where I didn't belong in their home anymore. It was time for me to reach out, and find my own life; my own home.

That evening, I ran into my high school friend, Pat. I don't know why, but I never saw her during the time we were in school or out of school. Just when we walked to school in the mornings, and yet she felt it was necessary to call us best friends, so I did. I really didn't care about labels. I spent a lot of time over Lawanda's house, and even more time with Trudy. I had different interest in all of them, so it didn't really matter, to me, who felt words were important. Anyway, I was walking to the club to determine where I was going to sleep that night, or should I say with whom, since I felt it was wrong to stay at my mom's sister's house. Pat told me I should stay over with her. Her mother wasn't going to be home, and besides, her mother loved me. Boy was that an understatement.

Pat and I sat around getting high; putting some chemicals called "Wash" in a baggie, and inhaling it. We paid five dollars for it. This was the latest crave. It came in a jar, and we would put some in a baggie, and breathe it in. We would damn near pass out but that was called getting high, and we couldn't wait to do it again. It was during this episode that Pat repeated the secret she had told me once when we were younger. Pat had been holding it inside about her mother, and father. He was a pimp, and her mother had been a prostitute for him. This is how she was conceived. Her mother hated men, and now dated women. Her mother was seeing one woman exclusively. This woman was the woman Pat introduced me to earlier as her Aunt Nancy.

I had told Pat about my situation so she told me that Nancy had a place right across the street, and I could ask her to stay there with her for awhile. Pat said, "She stays here most of the time anyway, so this would be a perfect solution." She continued, "We could stay over there, and they can stay with each other here." So, of course, when Pat's mom, and Nancy returned that night, we had it all planned. We talked to them about the plan. Nancy was the first to speak, "It is okay with me if you stay with me, but I'm not moving." This threw our plans out the window, even if it did give me a place to live.

I left with Nancy, and she showed me where I would sleep. Her place was nothing fancy. Definitely, not as large as my mom's house, but then my mom had lots more people living in her house. It kind of reminded me of our basement, it was so dark, and musky. But it was clean, warm, and it was snowing outside; so I wasn't about to be picky. I lay on the cot-like bed. I put my bag under it. As I was just about to go to sleep, I smelt liquor, prior to feeling someone on top of me. She was trying to get the blanket off my shoulders. It was Nancy. She had gone out, gotten drunk, and was now brave enough to do what she intended to do from the beginning. She kept repeating, "I can make you happy. I can make you feel real good." I jumped out of the bed, grabbed my bag and, with a few choice words, left Nancy's house.

I was about three blocks away before I realized, I was homeless again. I walked to the club most of the people I knew hung out. It was a dinky hole in the wall; but it was heaven to us. We 'ladies' would put on our makeup to look the age of twenty-one. No one was fooled, everyone knew everyone's age, but we just didn't care. The guys would buy the girls drinks, and eventually the girls would pick who they wanted, and go with them. This is how I got a place to stay that night. I met this tall guy, and we talked all night at the club. I didn't tell him I had nowhere to go. He was staying in the apartment of his friend, and his friend's lady. I didn't like him in the way I loved Kevin, but I needed a place to sleep, so I slept with him.

The next day, he followed me around like a puppy dog. In a way it was cute, but in another way it was getting on my nerves. I didn't love him like he wanted me too, but he wanted me so he made me feel guilty. Okay, I could live with guilt for a minute… I was still in high school, and I would be damned if I would let my mother feel like she was right about me. One time she told me, "You won't live to be twenty-one." Besides, an adult would finish their obligations. I went to school as much as I could. I worked twelve years for that diploma. So I walked across that stage to get it. Even if I did have to stay in his bed letting him have me every night for six months. The night I graduated from high school was the night, I left him. I walked up to my mother, father, and a couple of my brothers. I handed the diploma to my mother, and as I hugged her I said, "This belongs to you as much as it belongs to me. I love you mamma, I have to go now. Love you guys," I acknowledged my other family member's presence. I left to go with my friends that were waiting for me outside, in their ride.

After walking the streets, and jumping in, and out of several "necessary relationships," as I called them. I decided to move into a house with my sister, Paula. She had just given birth to two beautiful identical twin girls. One day Paula said to me, "Sissy, you do know that you too can have your own home? All you have to do is get pregnant." I replied, "But I want more with my life than to just have a baby, and my own home." I still wanted Kevin's baby but he didn't want one. I said, "I'm going to school to be better than I am, and make more money."

Paula came back with, "Oh, you think you're better than I am?" I said, "Paula, that is not what I'm saying, and you know it. I just think there is more out there to see, and do. I'm just not sure that the world I have now is all there is." That was the end of the conversation as I went back to play with the twins for hours. Paula was fun to live with. I didn't have to sleep around with strangers. I could go to the club when I wanted to. I'd go to work as I needed to, and stayed with her with only a low rent.

Define Friend

Before I worked at a nursing home, I tried to work at a Laundromat. This lasted about thirty minutes. After throwing those wet sheets around, and on top of the drying boards a few times, I thanked them for the experience. I politely told them to keep whatever money I might have coming to me. When I hastily left there, I knew what I didn't want to do with my life. That is when I applied for the nursing home position, and was hired.

I enjoyed this. I also was able to get a few hours of college in at the neighborhood college. My sister, Belinda allowed me to wear some of her clothes so I fit right in with the other college students. I didn't look as ghetto as I truly was. I really had a good time. I wasn't seeing Kevin as much as I was before, nor was I seeing anyone else. I was pretty much finished with men for right now. I was actually enjoying being me for me, for a change. So when I ran into Kevin, it was a pleasant surprise.

We walked, and talked about the past. Soon we were at the house I was sharing with Paula. It seemed so normal to walk into the house with him. Just as normal to find myself back in his arms again. After all the years we had been together, he definitely knew my body. I lay back as he caressed me as only he knew how. Kevin took off my clothing with the expertise of a man that knew a woman's body. He expertly took my blouse off with flair. I didn't even know it was off until I felt his warm hands on my breast. As he ran his hands down to my thighs, I opened up to him. Gladly my thighs allowed his manhood into me.

I asked Kevin so many times before to let me have his child. I knew it was my time of the month to get pregnant. I also knew the reasons

45

that he gave me were great ones. We both were too young, we both were in college, neither of us had anything to offer a child at this time. We didn't even live in our own apartment. I lived with my sister, and he lived with his grandmother. As the days went by I patiently waited, and started having sex with Kevin between my menstrual periods. He had no idea when my monthly was, like he used to, and he always went "bare back."

All that made sense to me was every time I saw him like this could almost certainly be my last chance to get pregnant by him. I so wanted the child of my first love. The night I conceived my first child, I knew I did, because of the connection I felt with my child; Kevin's child. The day I conceived, I was sure I was pregnant, when he left that day. I hadn't left much room for me not to be. I wanted Kevin's child so I was going to have it, even if I had no intention of letting him in on the miracle of my child's birth. I didn't see Kevin for awhile, nor did I have, as we called it, anyone else since I knew I was pregnant. I stopped seeing Kevin when I thought I might start showing. I didn't want to be a problem to Kevin. Kevin didn't want a child, so in my mind, he didn't get one. I would be mother, and father to this child. I would be strong enough for both. I would love this child enough for both of us.

When Belinda came to live with us, I was very happy. We were three sisters, and I was finally accepted in the group. Not for long. For some reason Belinda didn't want me around. She refused to let me wear her clothes anymore. This caused me to drop out of school because I would not go without something nice to wear. Then she kept lying to Paula about little things, petty nothings that all amounted to a big something. I finally told Paula, "I'm going to leave if you don't tell Belinda to go."

Paula said "I'm not going to tell Belinda to go, but you are free to leave." This is when I screamed at her, "Paula, I'm pregnant." She didn't believe me, Paula knew how I felt, or so I thought. "Sissy, you would do anything to get it your way. Of course, I'm not going to believe you. I'll give you until Friday to leave." I just couldn't believe she was sticking to her decision. She told me to go. I couldn't believe that after all Paula, and I had gone through; her having the twins while I was with her; babysitting whenever she wanted to go out, and providing money from my job at the nursing home every payday; I couldn't believe she was putting me out because Belinda wanted her too. I hadn't done anything to merit it, as far as I could see. It was Belinda that always initiated arguments about nothing.

Every morning, after morning sickness, I would get on the bus to the Department of Social Services (DSS) to apply for Aide for Dependent Children (AFDC). Of course I received it. It would seem this was my heritage. Paula taught me how to work the system. You get pregnant, than you apply. Once you are on welfare, the AFDC supply you with money for your apartment, food stamps, additional money for furniture, and a check until the time your child is of school age so you can get a job. If you're not ready to go to work, have another baby."

Well she was pretty much correct. As a matter of fact, in all of my schooling, that was the quickest, most efficient lesson on how to survive after high school. People say the people on welfare are lazy drug addicts. To tell you the truth, I was there, and I have to say, it was easy to get on welfare. I believe the system places these pitfalls in the path of our youth, and this garbage is being peddled by the negative role models. Although there are honest people in the world that try to ensure the youth a positive future; there are just not enough of them around.

When a young person is coming out of high school, or becoming a young adult, they need choices for their future that are just as clearly plotted as the welfare impasse. These young people are not lazy or stupid; they're scared, anxious, and intelligent. They're ready to follow someone that has achieved a successful future which they admire. What they need is guidance. They need guidance from positive role models, rather than negative role models. This is what I got, from my sister, totally negative. In my mind she had succeeded. She was surviving by the house she had, the babies she had, and the little bit of money seemed like a million dollars to someone like me. If she slept with anyone it was because she wanted to.

This was my reality. We definitely need more positive role models. The youth of America are just trying to survive. They want to have someone proud of them also, but survivors first. I left the day Paula asked me to be gone by; I stayed with William, a guy I knew before I stayed with Paula. At least until I could figure out what else to do. I believe I made my point about not going back to my mother's house. I remember when I stayed at my mom's house, and my sisters had left the house demonstrating the fact that they were grown, yet they always came back. My mom would laugh at them, and tell them that they were not as grown as they thought they were.

They also had to take the beating they were threatened with when they left. I swore to myself that it would never happen to me. Once I left, it would be for good. I would go for visits, but never to stay. William was a nice guy that had a huge crush on me. He stayed with his mother but it was in a situation that she didn't care if I was there. He was pretty big on PDA (Public displays of affections).

To tell the truth he was pretty big on affection period. The problem was I had a couple of issues with this. The first being he had this really bad smell on his body. I'm not sure where it came from, but being homeless, I was a little hesitant to tell him about it. Secondly, I'm not a touchy feely person. Alone or in public, there is a time, and place for everything. Third, and most importantly, I didn't like him personally, much less romantically. William was weak, and a momma's boy. I really didn't have much respect for him. When he kept putting his hands on me I would cringe, grit my teeth, and smile. I was quite the actress. I would listen to his dreams of our future together in another city for hours; like I would ever leave this state, or even this city, with him. William knew I was pregnant. That is one thing I have to say about this relationship. I didn't lie to him about that. He did know how I felt.

I told him from the beginning that the only reason I would consider his propositions was because I was pregnant, and homeless. I didn't come right out, and tell him he stunk, but he was a nice guy. He just wasn't for me. If I had discovered anything in this world, in my nineteen years, I have discovered the world is full of nice guys. It would seem this lifestyle was my legacy, if it wasn't for the fact that my father, who came from Florida, had twelve children, and worked for a corporation for years.

The corporation left the city to go south. Even this bump didn't change his attitude about never taking a dime of welfare. He was a very proud man, and he insisted that the responsibility to raise these twelve children was his. He refused to accept charity from anyone. It would have been impossible to move this big of a family. My father started collecting cans on the streets, and selling the aluminum. My father was a positive role model but he failed to talk to his children until well after it was too late in his and their lives.

Once I got my first welfare check, and was registered as an officially pregnant recipient, I left William, and his mother's house for my own. I refused to give them my new address for obvious reasons. I went shopping at the thrift stores for furniture with Pat; my girlfriend from school. I hadn't seen her in a long while. I just happened to run into her. I hadn't seen Kevin since I knew I was pregnant. He had no ideal I was pregnant, since he didn't want a baby, I felt he shouldn't get one. I decided to avoid him.

Life in the Fast Lane; 1971

It was 1971 when *"Simon and Garfunkel's Bridge Over Troubled Water,*[39]*"* won the Record of the Year award, *"All in the Family*[40]*"* debuted on CBS, *"Intel*[41]*"* introduced the microprocessor," which revolutioned computers, and the internet, *"Chat rooms*[42]*"* made their debut on the Internet, Charles Manson was convicted of murder, U.S. heavyweight thirty six year old, *"Sonny Liston's*[43]*"* corpse was found, there was a bomb attack on the *"Capitol in Wash DC,*[44]*"* the U.S. Supreme Court ruled unanimously that *"busing of students*[45]*"* may be ordered to achieve racial desegregation, *"Cigarette advertisements*[46]*"* were banned on TV, *"Barbra Streisand*[47]*"* appeared on The Burt Bacharach Special, on CBS TV, and last but truly not least, my son, Thomas L. Smith was born.

One night, I met a friend named Anthony, who agreed to help us, Pat, and me, move my furniture into my apartment the next day. Anthony and I were dating since the previous night, and I felt we might have a future. We moved the furniture up the two flights of stairs after we spent the whole day shopping. We were all so tired after we finished, the two of them started drinking beer. I knew better than to drink with my baby inside of me. Besides, I was just so tired I just lay across the bed, and passed out. I'm not sure what time it was when I woke up, but I didn't move when I did. I heard the moaning of my friends before I felt the bed moving. I couldn't believe what was happening. I had moved into a one bedroom apartment. It came with a living room and a kitchen.

Regardless of the demographics of my apartment, this was my best friend, and my man having sex in my bed; with me in it. I laid there a while, acting as if I were sleep. Trying to come up with a solution of what I should do. When they stopped moving; finished copulating right next to me, they went to sleep. I did not sleep the rest of the night. The next day I told them I heard them, and asked them to leave. Pat tried to protest, and plead her case, explain how it happened, but I really didn't want to hear it. I also just wanted to be left alone. I felt tired, and drained of feeling.

Sometimes looking back on the incident, I don't think the night before had much to do with my transition into a different lifestyle. I just knew I was pregnant now, and I was responsible for this living person inside of me. I knew there had to be a change in my lifestyle. Once they finally left I felt comfortable in the fact that my child, and I would be alright together. We didn't need Paula, Belinda, Pat or Anthony.

Thomas, and I sure as hell didn't need Kevin; in his world, and we would stand strong against the world out there. He didn't need a daddy. I was going to be strong enough to be both the mother, and the father. I patted my stomach, and promised my baby this was how it was going to be. I could go into numerous episodes of the times I spent pregnant, and going out alone or talk about the many nights, and days I stayed in my apartment alone, but I don't think that was a very interesting part of my life so I won't. I do remember when I went over to Paula's, house to stay since everyone insisted I should not be alone to have the baby. It just struck me as funny since that is exactly what happened.

I was sitting on the couch in the living room. No one else was home. When I heard a loud pop, it startled me at first. Then the sticky water started to ooze down my leg. I grabbed the closest thing to me, which turned out to be a brown paper bag. I put it between my legs, and waddled to the bathroom as fast as I could. I was only eight months pregnant so it was such a surprise for this to be happening. I didn't have any pain; I just had that damn fluid draining out of me. I had somehow grabbed the phone while I was running to the toilet, so I dialed 911. By the time my sisters returned home I was being loaded into the ambulance. I was in labor three days after that. The doctors said that due to the water coming out, it was very easy for the baby to get strangled with the umbilical cord.

Since this was the case, I could not get out of bed for any reason... especially not to go for a cigarette. Like I said there was still no pain, but when the pain did come, I assure you, I swore I was never going to do this again. When I looked into the eyes of my little boy; the man child I had been communicating my inner most thoughts, and dreams to for the last eight months, my heart just burst open with the love I had to give. I knew then I would protect this person from hell, and damnation for all eternity if need be. He was my son.

I wanted to take my son home, but again I agreed to do what the family thought would be best, which was to go to Paula's house with Thomas. I would not be alone. They weren't so concerned about me to come see me at the hospital. There is nothing worse than to have a beautiful baby boy, and no one to show him too. I felt so all alone. I felt fine from the word go, so when I got home I thought nothing of walking to Monica's house to show her the baby.

When I got there, she had a taxi waiting for me to take back to Paula's house. She must have called after I left, and Paula told her I was walking to her house two days after having the baby. She was very upset. She said, "Girl if you're trying to kill yourself, take another step toward this house, I'm going to kill you myself. Get in that cab and go back home, I already paid him. Sissy, you are going to be the dealt of me."

Monica resided on the second floor so she said, "If you come up these stairs, I will personally kill you myself." I responded with, "Monica, I will get in the cab. See I'm in the cab. I am so sorry; I didn't know what I was thinking. You're right, you're right, and I am so sorry. I just wanted you to see my baby." Since there were two flights of stairs up to her apartment, and I had just walked a mile to her house. She was leaning out of her window. I tried to get a word in, but she wasn't having it…" I don't care how good you feel, child, you just had a baby three days ago, you are wide open… Get in that cab, and take your ass to bed, with that baby. Child if you don't get in that cab… you will be the death of me yet." I really hadn't thought about it that way, not that I had a choice; I went back to Paula's house, and got back in bed.

I pretty much stayed with Paula, going back and forth between my apartment, and hers. I had named my son Thomas. When he was six weeks old Paula and I went out to celebrate. As usual, we went to a bar of her choosing since I really didn't know any place in her neighborhood. I remember talking to this woman who kept trying to tell me what she could do with her tongue to me. I was not interested. She insisted, "Girl if you tried me, you would never go back to men." I told her, "That is exactly what I'm afraid of, so go away." I didn't realize it then, but she was the least of my problems.

I got up, and went across the street to that bar where Paula had left me; she still wasn't there. I sat at the bar awaiting her return, when this tall rather thick man stepped up to me, and asked, "May I buy you a drink." Not being one to turn down a free drink, I said, "Of course." He sat next to me, and we talked for a while. He seemed nice enough, but he really wasn't my type. That being said, I never really got over Kevin. It was only six weeks since my baby was born, and I really wasn't ready to get involved with anyone, free drinks or not....

It seemed like hours had passed but Paula still had not returned, so I decided to go home. I tried to excuse myself, nicely, only now this bumbling idiot wanted to walk me home. I told him it was a free world, and I turned to leave. He got up to follow me. I'm not sure how long we had been walking, or what I said to get this started, but the next thing I know he was half pulling, half picking me up to get me in a back yard, and on the ground. I wanted to scream, but I could hardly breathe. As he removed his hand away from my mouth, I felt the cold smooth metal of a knife against my neck. He told me, "If you scream I will cut your throat."

He took the knife, and lowered it down to my panties, cutting them off with one surf movement. The knife was back at my throat before I even realized it had been gone. The assailant lowered his hands to examine the prize he had so recently set free. He lowered his body, so he could smell my aroma so fresh after only six weeks of delivering a child. He started to lick me down below, over, and over again. I heard him muttering, pleading about never letting some woman go, how we would always be together like this, how much he loved to eat me. If this situation wasn't so dangerous; I do believe I would feel sorry for him, he seemed so pitiful. But this guy had a rather large knife at my throat, and it didn't look like he loved me enough to put it down. My mind was spinning, trying to collect all my wits about myself to ensure I successfully came out of this situation, alive. I had a newborn baby who I promised I would be there for.

I took a deep breath, and swallowed my pride; acting like I was having just as many organisms as he was, I assured him we would be together forever. When he finished, he put the knife in his side pocket. Although I believed he thought I was with him, in love with him now, he wasn't taking any chances of me getting away. When we were about to go pass a favorite eating place of my friends; I told him I was hungry. By now he was willing to do anything for me. As we went in I frantically looked around. Unfortunately there were none of my close friends out tonight. When we came upon a booth, he insisted I get into the booth first. The night was getting on when in walked an acquaintance, named Rico. I never did know what his real name was, but Rico was a small white man that hung around with a group of my friends. Although he was the only white in this area, nobody thought to mess with him. He was small in stature, but big in backbone; people did not mess with him; some say he's just nuts, but he was always nice to me. He was alone tonight, but if I was going to get out of this mess, it would seem it would have to be through him. As he came into the diner, he didn't see me at first, but when I thought my rapist wasn't looking, I gestured to Rico to help me…

I think he caught the fear in my eyes because he came over, and said, "Woman, where in hell have you been all night? Bitch I been looking for my money all night, and who the hell is this?" I was so shocked, I didn't know what to say, so I just kept it simple too, and said, "He's just a guy, but I was looking for you too, baby." My assailant didn't know what was going on so he pretty much let me out of the booth to talk with my pimp. I'm sure by the time he figured out what just happened. Rico and I were long gone, and out of the neighborhood. It was about at this point in time when I pretty much decided not to go out to clubs to meet guys anymore. I did take my assailant to court, and he is doing time in a federal penitentiary, a fifth teen to twenty year term. After the rape incident, it was pretty easy to live with the decision to stay out of the bars.

What's Going on at Home

The first time I went out, since the rape, I met Dennis, a man that had just gotten out of prison after he had committed an armed robbery with a group of guys, at the age of twenty-one. Listening to Dennis talk, you would think those were his proudest moments. The ones he spent in jail with the boys. Anyway, one night I was at the club, being very bored. He was sitting at the other end of the bar. He came over, told me his name, and we became best buddies from that moment on. There was no special lighting; no glitter, bells ringing or gimmicks…

It was a relationship based on a true honest to goodness friendship. Others around us made such an effort to make it more but we knew how we felt. I needed his help taking care of Thomas; he needed my help to stay out of jail, and away from living with his father. I was on the government's AFDC program already so I didn't need anyone else's financial assistance. He moved in with no benefit of ceremonial concern. One day he left a sweater in my home; another day his shaving attire was in my bathroom. It never accrued to me to ask him for rent, to leave or stay. We just continued being friends.

One day Kevin caught-up with me (so to speak). I was sitting on my porch when he walked up. He sat down next to me, asking "How have you been?" I had been reading the newspaper so I knew he had joined the military, and was stationed somewhere close to New York. He had returned home because he was scheduled to marry Nona this Saturday. I answered him with a lump in my throat, "I've been okay, and you?" He continued, "I've been looking for you." I answered, "Why, would you look for me?" He continued, "Oh I don't know, maybe it's because I feel that you've been avoiding me."

I was beginning to feel trapped, like a caged animal with nowhere to go, "Kevin, why would I avoid you? Maybe that's just your ego talking to you." Kevin said this without the usual smile on his face, "I need to know something and I want you to be honest with me. Is your son ours?" I was shocked, "Kevin, where are you getting all of this from?" I thought I had been so careful. How could he know? I said, "Have you lost your mind. Besides you're here to marry Nona, Saturday." I held my breath; I had not wanted him to know I knew. "Sissy, if the baby has you and me in him, I swear I will not marry her Saturday. I will marry you today. You know I love you. Always did." I could not believe my ears. "Kevin I can't believe I am hearing the words I have always wanted you to say. But, now you are about to marry Nona, you came to town specifically to marry her. I live with Dennis; I love you and always will, but I can't wreck other peoples' hearts because you think I have your son. I wished it were true Kevin, but he's not your son. You go ahead and marry Nona, our time has passed. What we had was "splendor in the grass.[48]" But thank you for finally saying what I needed to hear years ago. I also will always love you too."

I turned, and went into the house locking the door. I wasn't afraid he would come in, I was afraid I would run out to him, and jump into his arms. Telling him, "Yes, yes, yes Kevin. Thomas is your son, I lied, and he is your son. Yes I will marry you; to hell with all of these other people. I love you, and I always will." But I did care; I didn't want to begin our new life together by hurting others. I didn't want to start our marriage on the pain of others.

It hurt me like hell, but I couldn't do it. Especially the pain of telling him Thomas was not his son. I had made a promise to Thomas that it would be me and him forever. How stupid I was. Kevin left, and I haven't seen him again. I don't know whether he married Nona or not. Our day had come and gone. I pray I made the right decision; if not for me than for Thomas. Dennis and my friendship grew into what we believed was love. Dennis would try to help as much as he felt he could, but as he put it (repeatedly), he was a felon, and nobody wanted to hire a felon. I was on welfare when I met him, and I was on welfare when I left him, four years later.

Throughout my marriage, I remember him bringing very little to the table. In my effort to ensure food was on the table, I remember, the days when we not only sold marijuana, but I would get dressed up, with Dennis watching. He knew I was going out to get money from some man in any way I had to. This was our lifestyle, and it seemed as normal as getting up in the morning. Having a passion for marijuana is the reason I must say, "It was just a small stepping stone for me to use stronger illegal drugs, and enter the world of madness."

Marijuana was a drug that numerous groups, and thousands of Americans use with only one thought in mind, that being; "A need to legalize it." In the middle seventies, I got caught up in not only using marijuana, but also selling it. This was initiated by my husband, of course, who seemed to fail at getting, as well as keeping, legitimate employment. Selling marijuana supplemented our income, which was helpful along with the AFDC program, and my going out in the night. Once I had it in my mind that using marijuana was normal, and it was okay to smoke marijuana since everybody else was using it. I had no problem giving marijuana to my brothers as they came to me for it. I never sold it to them. I gave it to them. I would even give marijuana to them, and have them watch my babies; knowing they were going to get high.

Subconsciously, I knew that I couldn't justify using marijuana, but using it made it easier to justify using other drugs. Drugs that were illegal, such as marijuana, held a lesser risk of going to jail. Although it hinders some users' health problems, a lot of users of marijuana try to justify medical value in it. All this was because the use of marijuana was seen as important to many a users' lifestyle. No matter how many people were in the news for being; arrested, or fined, or both, for getting caught in possession of drugs. It never seem to get through to users' that they would or could either get caught, and serve time, or get ensnared into addiction of other harder drugs.

Back then I believed it couldn't happen to me; which is the same sickness many of us had. I was not alone; since many felt the high we received was too great for us to care about the consequences. Getting high was a way of life for those around me. I realistically knew that getting arrested or becoming further addicted to other drugs could happen to anyone. It was understood that no one told our parents about this secret. This, in itself, tells you we knew we were doing wrong. No one questioned our way of life, nor asked for permission to be in it. This came naturally with the ability to hold a joint to the lips with no one around saying no. It was a rite of passage in our neighborhood.

No one asked to be in this neighborhood, but one had to fight to get out. Only a few did get out. There are only a few ways that one got out. The ones to get out usually were the ones that studied in school until they were old enough to go to college, the ones that joined the military, or the few that had relatives that lived in a different lifestyle. Sometimes the neighborhood followed them out. A person who has been successful in escaping the effects of and need to use drugs sometimes went back into addictive behavior. I felt that I was one of the people that would never get out. It never occurred to me that Dennis should protect me from this life. As a matter of fact sometimes it seemed like it was my responsibility to protect Dennis.

There was no need to come right out to form the words; words that would only castrate him further. Dennis would explain to me about the system. "The establishment has done a great job of keeping the poor man down, throwing them in jail consequently making them felons. Keeping the men away from higher education and the good jobs... not to mention placing the indigent women in charge of the household as a result castrating their men." Dennis would further explain to me all about the system. "Whether it is by the men being in jail or the women who needed the assistance of the welfare system.

Aid to Dependent Children (ADC) was designed to provide financial consideration to the females, and children in need, while castrating the indigent men." Thereby, breaking down the family structure, the men are not allowed to reside in the household. This vicious cycle continues for years as the male child is raised by the females to believe this lifestyle is a true depiction of how it is supposed to be." Dennis was always quick to deliver his version of American history. Dennis constantly beat the thoughts into my mind that it was the establishment that placed us in this position; not himself. He could find no work, there was no food, and we were not going to ask our parents.

Dennis' father, and brother, and all of our friends wanted us to get married but we didn't see the rush. It was quite apparent that we were a couple, but we didn't believe in the ties that the establishment felt was necessary for a couple to have. One weekend we were in the next room where we heard an argument between our closest friends; Paul and Nancy, it seemed, were about to call it quits on their marriage. They were legally married, and had three boys aging from six to ten. They were our icon of the perfect marriage, if there ever was one in Dennis, and my dysfunctional minds. This was the reason Dennis and I got married. We decided that we would travel to Chicago, Illinois, where they lived, to tell them about the marriage. They along with the other friends that lived in Chicago, and our friends that lived in Milwaukee would all come together in Waukesha, Wisconsin, where there was no waiting period.

It was such a lovely wedding that everything worked out perfectly. Paul and Nancy most have felt the romance of it also because there was no longer any talk of divorce. In the end, yes Dennis and I were married, but I really must say it was for the event itself, rather than the normal reasons. By this time in my life, I learned to depend on myself. I just took the AFDC check. I was still getting a monthly check, which I needed. Once Dennis and I got married we were the epitome of the song, "Break Up, to Make Up.[49]" The only thing was we didn't just break up, we fought. Sometimes it seemed like we hated each other, but I was not the type to get hit, and then leave it alone. If I got hit, I hit back, knowing all along I was going to end up on the losing side.

One day I remember going over to my mother's home, forgetting that I still had bruises. My father was home so he saw my black eye. He asked me, "What happened to your eye?" I thought about it two seconds before I lied, "I was looking for something in the bathroom when I opened the cabinet, and ran into the edge of the door." My dad looked at me a minute, then said, "Okay, but I'm not going to hear about too many more of those cabinets stories. If I ever find out that bastard is hitting you, I will kill him." I looked into his eyes, and realized he meant what he was saying.

It just stuck me as odd that he would beat my mother all these years, but he was upset about my husband hitting me. I said, "I understand Daddy." But I really didn't. The one thing Dennis did give me was

59

the most beautiful daughter in the world. From the moment I laid eyes on this baby with long silky curls, and a button nose, her bright eyes sparkling, and full of happiness, I knew she would be something special in my life. I cherished this child in such a way, only God could understand how much. I named her Deidre and we called her Dee.

A Meeting of the Minds; 1974

It was 1974 when due to the *"Watergate Scandal,[50]"* U.S. President Richard Nixon announced his resignation (effective August 9), the Rumble in the Jungle took place in Kinshasa, Zaire, where *"Muhammad Ali[51]"* knocked out George Foreman in eight rounds to regain the heavyweight title, which had been stripped from him seven years earlier, and after a record eighty four days in orbit, the crew of *"Skylab 4[52]"* returned to Earth. I had completed my training class, and the school had placed me in my new job. Thomas was an only child for a long time. He, being three years senior to the new baby girl, my concerns, were put to rest. It seemed as if they had been together from the start. Thomas took it upon himself to care for his baby sister. He did this without being told to do so. It was as if he knew this was his job. They got along so beautifully.

Did I blame Dennis for his inability to be the man I had expected him to be? Resent him for not being a stronger man that would protect me from the streets? I will never really know the answer to those questions. I never really got the chance to decide it was his fault. As I saw it, even he bought the hype. The real situation was he robbed the establishment with a gun, for no good reason, I might add, since he came from a well to do family, and he was just trying to show off to the fellows. He was the one that did not apply for the jobs because it was easier to say he was being oppressed. He wanted to feel like he was a pimp in the eyes of his friends, even if it's just his wife he was pimping. In my mind, again, it was as normal for me to believe the reasons why I was a prostitute as it was to get on AFDC when I got pregnant with

Thomas. I knew this lifestyle was detrimental to my longevity so I started looking for ways out.

I started going to a technical college which ensured employment upon graduation. When I started working at the city hall, in the Tax Commissioner's Office, I was so proud of myself. All Dennis had to do was watch the two children while I was at work. One day when I returned home from work for lunch; I had brought them surprise sandwiches. Thomas, a four year old, was in the living room with Dee, who was little more than one year old, sitting on the couch in front of the television. I asked, "Thomas, where's Daddy?"

He responded, "Daddy always leaves after you leave. I always get Dee up in front of the television because it stops her from crying." I sat down on the floor next to the couch where they sat. I prepared, and handed the food to them. They ate as if they were starving. As tears welled up in my eyes, I realized that life as I knew it had passed again. A new episode was coming into view. I could no longer trust Dennis, especially with my most prize possessions.

Thomas looked at me with those big brown trusting eyes, asking me "Am I in trouble mamma? Did I do good?" You could tell by his demeanor that he wanted to know if he did the right thing in telling me. I told him, "Thomas, you know you always do good in my eyes. Don't you ever worry about telling me the right thing? You tell me anything you want too. I'm your mamma, and I love you, okay? You are my little man, and I think you did great."

Dennis came into the door about now. It was time for me to put on my façade again. I had to go back to work, and telling Dennis I was upset could serve absolutely no purpose at this time. I smiled, and said, "Hey baby" I cheerfully explained, "I was trying to surprise you guys with lunch, your sandwich is on the stove." Handing Dennis the rest of the sandwiches I had just fed the children I told him, "I'll see you, love, when I get off work."

I thought he bought the act, but apparently not, because when I returned, later that evening, I had just gotten off the bus, and was walking down the street toward my home when I noticed the little boy running toward me was Thomas. As he neared I could see the onset of a black-eye. I reached for him, and screamed, "What happened to your eye?" He started to really cry now that he was in my arms. "Mama, if I tell you, will you please promise you won't tell Daddy?"

I said, "What, do you mean, if you tell me? Of course you're going to tell me. What happened to your eye, and where are Daddy, and Dee?" He was frantic when he said, "When you left, Daddy got mad at me, and said I talk too much. Then he hit me. He told me if I told you he was going to kill me." I reached down, and grabbed my son in my arms. I hugged him ever so tightly. I cried for his pain, wondering what I had gotten us into. I assured him, "Thomas, you will never have to worry about Dennis or anyone else killing you or hitting you again." After I got him to stop crying I told him to go ahead, and continue to play outside with his friends.

I got up from the porch step I was sitting on, and started walking up the flight of stairs to my own home. I wasn't sure what I was going to say. I knew that Dennis was at the top of the stairs; in the apartment, waiting for my return home. I was sure he was on the defense since I believed what Thomas said. I really didn't know how I was going to handle this, since I had grown to love Dennis, but no man had the right to hit my child, much less, leave them alone all day. When I walked into the apartment Dennis was perched on a kitchen chair, upside down, on his head.

Deidra was in her crib asleep, and Thomas was outside playing with his friends. There was no real urgency for me to worry about the children just then. I walked over to him, and asked, "Dennis, what are you doing?" He then said, "I'm meditating, so when the Klan comes, I'll know what to do." "Are you serious?" I asked. "Do you realize that it's almost six o'clock, and you haven't even started cooking dinner?" He answered me with, "Yeah, well you better start cooking, since I have better things to worry about than eating.

Do you realize that Whitey is about to attack us any day now, and we have to get ready? Do you want to die? Woman! Don't bother me with such trivial things like dinner. I have to think of a way to save this family from the disaster." Seeing him, perched upside down on the chair, and while he spoke to me solidified my decision to leave him. I had been so busy transitioning into my newfound lifestyle that it never donned on me that my family might have needed my attention also.

For the first time in weeks I looked at him; really looked at him. Dennis had changed his appearance. He had cut off all of his hair, the mustache he normally wore was no longer there, and although he normally had a thin physique; he was really thin now. How could I not notice all of these differences? I had started going back to school every day early in the morning, and returning late in the evening, I was so busy trying to adjust to the people, and the new schedules, when this new situation with Dennis, and the children started; it was a devastating blow when I discovered my family was in crisis. This situation was definitely causing me to once again, rethink my value system.

After the completion of the IBM Course, I was chosen to work at the city hall, in the Tax Commissioner's Office. I worked on the keypunch machines in the basement floor. It was tedious work, but I felt so proud to be earning my own money, rather than depending on the Welfare Department's AFDC to feed my family. I was truly my father's daughter, because even though I could have settled for the pennies dished out, I just couldn't do it. I wanted so much more for my children.

I knew there had to be more out there than what I was getting, and I had to struggle to find it. I owed my children that much. I knew I owed it to myself also. I hated sleeping with total strangers for money. I am no fool; I knew that living this way would eventually bring me nothing more than sickness, more shame, jail or death. I owed them so much more. I would die before I settled for the lifestyle I had grown so familiar with. As my children grew up, not only would they learn of my lifestyle, but this would eventually have to be their starting point, as it had been mine. I couldn't let that happen. I wanted so much more for them.

A Walk into Madness; 1975

It was 1975, the end of the *"Vietnam War,*[53]*"* one of the true success stories of modern times was how *"Bill Gates*[54]*"* and Paul Allen created the company Microsoft, and the average cost of a new home was "thirty nine thousand, and three hundred dollars." I was in deep thoughts of my children when I pulled my thoughts back to Dennis, who by now had gotten off of the chair, and was seated at the kitchen table.

Putting my attention back on Dennis I listened to his ranting once again. I interrupted him to say, "Okay, I'm going to cook dinner tonight, what do you want to eat?" He answered me, but I could tell he really wasn't listening to me. "Nothing, I'm fasting, I need to cleanse my body of all that Whitey has put in the food we eat." I had no idea what he was talking about, nor did I care. My mind was running at one hundred miles an hour, trying to determine how I was going to get out of that house without him starting a fight. Dennis and I had many fights that ended in my bruises or cuts.

I still had never asked to come home. As a matter of fact, my father had told me under no uncertain terms, "If I ever find out this guy is hitting you, I can guarantee you, he won't be doing it again; to you or nobody else." I swore to him, "Daddy I ran into the cabinet. I don't have a reason to lie to you." I just didn't want any trouble between my husband, and my father. Dennis and I fought some before we got married, but it got worse. We had serious arguments after our wedding. Now it seems like that's all we did. I felt like this was my problem to deal with, so I didn't see the point in telling my parent, or anyone else;

my problems. It also struck me as peculiar that my father felt so strong against a man putting his hands on one of his daughters.

I can still remember the night when I was sleeping in the downstairs bedroom. My bedroom was just off from the landing of stairs, which went to the upstairs bedrooms. I heard my mother's loud voice, yelling at him about something. He retorted with a comment which was laced with several well chosen curse words. The next thing I heard was a very loud slap, which I wasn't sure was my father hitting my mother until she came falling down the stairs, head first. I knew then for sure that it was daddy hitting my mom, and I was sure at this time that he would have hit her again, if he hadn't thought he killed her by the fall down the stairs.

I pulled the covers tighter to my neck. I acted like I was still asleep so they didn't catch me peeking. By the time she landed on the bottom stair, he was there. They were at the bottom of the stairs hugging, with both of them crying. Daddy was trying to comfort momma by swearing how he didn't mean it, and he would never do it again. My momma was saying she loved him, and how she was okay. They left the room, getting ready to go to bed. I could tell that both of them were drunk.

This is only one incident of their many drunken escapades, which were witnessed by me or at least one of my other siblings. Since they have gotten older, it seems, they have either settled down or just gotten tired. I have witnessed them going through many of their escapades prior to me moving out years later; none of my siblings have mentioned anything they have witnessed. I suppose there was an unwritten rule. It is just so condescending to hear my father talking like someone who cares about women's rights. Daddy acts like someone that knows it is wrong to hit a woman, for any reason. "What about my *Mother!*"

When I got to my mother's house, I explained to her, "Momma, I just need to stay long enough to get a place for us to stay." I didn't have to say much, since one; she saw Thomas' black eye, and two; she never liked Dennis to begin with. My father liked him even less, if you can imagine. It wasn't as hard to go back home as I thought it would be. But I was twenty-four now, and I had two children, but at least I had a job.

I'm not going to even mention an estranged husband. I got a phone call from Dennis' father, Mr. James, as I called him, one day about two weeks after I had left Dennis. He wanted me to come over his house to talk. I really didn't want to, but I agreed to do so. He had gotten married to Ms Cathy after Dennis' mother, Ms. Louise, had finally called it quits, and ran off to California. When she left, she took her youngest daughter with her. The house was left to her, by her grandmother, but she gave it to Mr. James, just to ensure a clean, quick divorce.

Mr. James always treated me like a special person in his life. He always said I was too good for his son. I hated when he started talking like that because it was never long before he would start talking about if he was a few years younger, or if he met me first. I know he meant well, he always made me feel so uncomfortable to be around him. He would make these comments around Ms. Cathy, Dennis, Dennis' brother Reggie and anyone that would listen. It didn't bother Mr. James who it embarrassed. He always said exactly what he was thinking, without thinking.

I arrived at Mr. James' house early in the afternoon. Ms. Cathy, his wife, let me in, and then returned back to the kitchen after greeting me. Mr. James was sitting in the screened in porch. He looked very serious, and very sad. I saw the cast on his leg and wondered how that happened. I kissed him on his cheek in greeting, and sat down beside him. I felt that this conversation had something to do with Dennis, but since he called me I was going to let him initiate this conversation.

I've never been one to tell our troubles to our parents. "Have you seen Dennis recently?" he began the dialogue. "No, I haven't seen him in two weeks. Not since I left him to move in with my mom." Mr. James stated "You have to help my son. I don't know what to do, but he needs help. He done lost his mind. He's walking around in twenty below zero degree weather with no coat; I gave him a leather coat, and somebody told me they saw him burying it in the snow. He's wearing sandals in the winter time. If you talk to him, you will see for yourself that he makes no sense.

Please Sissy, please help me to help him. I just can't talk to him, and we never could get along anyway." He didn't say anything about his relationship with his son that I didn't already know. He continued, "It was just a week ago when Dennis came by here to visit. I was trying to talk to him, when we got into a heated argument, and the next thing I knew, I was rolling down the hill in front of this house." That incident ended with Mr. James having this broken leg.

I listened to his plea. I also reminisced about the good times Dennis and I had together. We had been together a total of four years prior to this situation. So many times we had each others' back. Now it was my turn to take a position. I thought about the last couple of days prior to my departure from our home. It all started to make sense. Dennis' loss of control over his mind made the whole incident understandable now.

Thomas' black eye; Dennis standing on his bald head on the kitchen chair; cutting up his clothes together now. I told his father, "I will make an attempt to talk to Dennis. I don't know what I'm getting into, but I feel that if it were me needing his help he would be there for me." I didn't want to raise Mr. James' hopes. I still loved Dennis and I knew he still loved me. I knew nothing about the human mind, but I knew I didn't want anything to happen to Dennis. I didn't know for sure how I would go about it either. I went back to my mother's house, and told her what Mr. James had told me.

Momma wasn't keen on the idea of me going back into that house, but she was happy that I had enough sense not to take the children back with me. "I told you something was wrong with that boy a long time ago. None of yawl would believe me." "Momma, he was fine before. He is just going through a rough patch, that's all." My mother said, "Okay rough patch. You take your ass own up there. The next time I'm gonna see you will be when they put you in a box. I'll bet you wish you'd a believed me then. You just leave my babies here. Take your ass on up there by yourself." I returned, "Momma, do you have to be so dramatic? It's not going to come to that. I'm just going to talk to him. I need to try to see if I can do anything to help."

The next day I walked up the stairs to our apartment. I was wondering if he was home. I wasn't looking forward to him being there. As I unlocked the door I could see he had remodeled the living room. The curtains were no longer hanging on the windows. In their place were the dark blankets that use to be on the beds. The kitchen chairs were upside down holding the doors to ensure no entry in the event the locks didn't work. It was very dark in the house so at first sight it didn't dawn on you how much rubbish was on the floors. Dishes were stacked in the sink area in such a way that you would think I had been gone more than two weeks.

He wasn't home, which was probably why my key alone got me into the house. I went into the kitchen, and started to turn around, and leave; it was that bad. Instead, I decided to clean the kitchen, or at least make a good go at it. As I was finishing up the kitchen Dennis walked into the house. He looked like hell.

He now kept the hair on his head shaved off, the sandals his father saw were actually his regular street shoes he had cut up to look like sandals, he had cut his slacks to create a Bermuda shorts effect, he was now sporting a mustache, and beard; which I never saw him wear before. He had a pair of shades he wore; whenever he left the house. The shirt he wore was also altered, so of course it was raggedy. I couldn't believe all this took place after I left, only two weeks ago.

Helter Skelter; 1976

It was 1976, the *"Apple Computer Company[55]"* was formed by *"Steve Jobs and Steve Wozniak[56],"* the democrats nominated former Georgia, Governor, *"Jimmy Carter[57]"* in their convention at New York's, Madison Square Garden, the U.S. pitted incumbent *"President Gerald Ford,[58]"* the republican candidate against the relatively unknown." It was the presidential election of 1976, which followed the resignation of President Richard Nixon, in the wake of the Watergate scandal. In the meantime back at the farm, there was Dennis.

Dennis stood in the kitchen doorway looking at me like he didn't believe I was really there. "Dennis, so you made it home. I don't suppose you have time to help clean up this mess?" He walked over to me like he was perplexed, as well as distrustful. I could tell by his demeanor that he didn't understand why I was back, but he was glad and didn't want to do anything to jeopardize losing me again.

He started the conversation with, "Where are the children?" I answered, "Over Mom's house, their fine over there until we talk. You do know we have a problem, and we need to work it out, right?" I added, he acknowledged "Yeah, maybe we do, but it's because you won't recognize the reality of the prejudices in America." "Dennis, I'm not to blame for our marriage breaking down, any more than America's reality is at fault for our marriage breaking down. You're talking apples and oranges." After I cleaned up the kitchen, while he talked, I cooked dinner.

Dennis continued to dialog about Charles Manson. He had gotten hold of the book, and while I laid down that night trying to sleep, he sat next to me reading chapters from it all night. I finally had to ask him, "Dennis, I don't understand something. If we are going to war, as black people, with Manson as our leader, isn't he white?" "That is what they want you to believe. Manson's father was black. That's why Manson's such a good musician, and so charismatic."

I thought to myself, "That's what I get for trying to put holes in his precious Helter, Skelter theory." I tried to clarify to him, "Dennis do you believe he talked all those people into being members of his "family," convincing them he was a modern day reincarnation of Jesus Christ. I was told he had ulterior motives; he figured he could benefit in some way by starting a race war in America." I continued "Manson convinced those people to follow him because he knew they were weak; he was trying to get blacks, and whites to think black people did that murderous spree in 1969, during which they killed Sharon Tate, and six other people. In this way they would start a racial riot."

"Well, Dennis, you know what happened to him, and the people that followed him. The subsequent murder trial lasted seven months (at this time the longest, and most expensive in US history), and resulted in guilty verdicts, and death sentences for Manson, and his followers. In 1972, California outlawed the death penalty, and Manson was sentenced instead to life in prison. Is that what you want to happen to this family?"

He angrily replied "No, but anything that isn't worth dying for isn't worth having." I don't know how it was possible, with all the drama going on but I finally gave up, and fell asleep. Dennis was running around acting like a black panther, a wannabe Manson follower. Dennis's father was continuously calling to cry, and beg me to help his son. He didn't want Dennis to come into his home again, he couldn't control him. His attitude was rightfully assumed. The last time Dennis went by his father's house, they had gotten into an altercation which ended in his father having a broken leg. I really couldn't blame him for not wanting Dennis to come by his home.

They both had some pretty deep seated issues they should have worked on many years ago. Yet instead of facing the issues when they first surfaced, his father sent him away to New York, when he was fourteen years old to live with relatives. As time went on Dennis' mental problems became stronger, taking over his everyday life. Of course, when this happened his father, who couldn't deal with the antics of a fourteen year old son, was not going to be sympathetic to a seventeen year old who had just gotten in trouble with the law, with an armed robbery charge.

I told Dennis, "We need to see a marriage counselor." I was really taking him in to see a psychiatrist. I knew he still loved me, I still loved him. I just wished the shell that was him these days would let him out to be with me sometimes. I guess I'm trying to say, I realized that the man I loved no longer existed. This erratic copy of my husband that answered to his name was not Dennis. I never knew from day to day (sometimes moment to moment), what this person was going to do. He had agreed to go to a marriage counselor, as long as I understood that it was my fault that we were not in communicating. He said, "I love you enough to go wherever you need us to go to get fixed."

I spoke to Dennis about this marriage counselor, and upon completion of the session with the psychiatrist; Dr. Miles said he wanted to talk to us as individuals. I wasn't sure what he was doing since he didn't confide in me prior to the meeting, but I did know that I had to trust the man to do his job. Dennis was definitely in trouble mentally, and I was ill equipped to help him. After about an hour, I was told to come in, and Dennis was told to wait outside in the lobby. It was my turn to talk to him. Dr. Miles didn't hesitate to tell me what the problem was. "Your husband suffers from an illness called paranoid schizophrenia."   •

Dr. Miles went on to say, "Schizophrenia is a chronic, severe, and disabling mental illness. It affects men and women with equal frequency. People suffering from schizophrenia may have symptoms such as delusions, false personal beliefs, held with conviction in spite of reason or evidence to the contrary. These things are not explained by that person's cultural context or hallucinations, perceptions can be sound, sight, touch, smell, or taste." He went on to say, "The occurrence is, in the absence of an actual external stimulus, auditory hallucinations. Those of voice or other sounds are the most common type of hallucinations in schizophrenia."

I really didn't understand what all this meant. I just wanted to know, "How did he get it? Will he get better?" Dr. Miles answered me with, "Schizophrenia is usually diagnosed in people of many ages.

The illness appears earlier in men in their late teens or early twenties. Women are usually affected in the twenties to early thirties. Dennis probably showed signs of it in his youth. It's normal for people with this affliction to have relapses. They can go through periods when they seem quite normal after having an onset. Many of them are disabled. They may not be able to hold down jobs or even perform tasks as simple as conversations.

Some may be so incapacitated that they are unable to do activities most people take for granted, such as showering or preparing a meal. Many are homeless. Some recover enough to live a life relatively free of assistance." "Dennis was diagnosed as a paranoid schizophrenia, which is characterized by delusions, and auditory hallucinations, but relatively normal intellectual functioning, and expression of affect. The delusions can often be about being persecuted unfairly, or being some other person who is famous. People with paranoid-type schizophrenia can exhibit anger, aloofness, anxiety, and argumentativeness. This is why Dennis wants to go out into the suburbs, and kill off all the honkeys."

When Dr. Miles said this, I was embarrassed, since Dr. Miles was a white man. Yet since he didn't seem to react to it, I soon relaxed about it, and continued to listen. "Dennis feels a real need in his mind to protect his family, and to do what is best for America. He also loves you, and he says, his wife won't let him do what he knew he had to do. With that love, you can assist us to get him the help he needs. It will take two weeks to get a bed in the hospital for him.

If you leave him, I don't know whether he will go off, and accomplish what he wants to, which is 'to go off into the suburbs, and kill all the honkeys. Of course, we would prefer for him to stay at home with you for two weeks until we can get him the help he needs." Dr. Miles continued with, "But I must warn you that although right now you are his control. There are no guarantees. He may wake up in the middle of the night, or tomorrow, and decide to kill you instead. So with all this in mind, what do you want to do?" I jokingly said, "Run away, and hide."

The Early Years

As I went home with my husband I wondered how Dr. Miles thought I could say anything other than, "Of course I will stand by my man." Dennis was not alone in his love for me, I loved him also. Our love may have started from a friendship, but it developed into a genuine love. We both had gone through so much in this relationship that I felt I owed it to him, as his wife, to be there for him. Ethically and morally I knew I could never live with myself if I didn't make every effort to help him.

Of course I did not tell him what really transpired in the doctor's office. Since the psychiatrist explained it would take two weeks to get Dennis a placement into the mental facility, and/or getting a court hearing declaring him incompetent to handle his own affairs, it was useless to arm him with more than he could handle. The doctor also indicated that we would need three signatures to declare him incompetent. I knew his father would be one; of course I could do it but that third signature was a problem.

After I got him home, and settled in, I told him I needed to go to my mom's to see the children. He said that was fine since he had some things to do also. He rarely spoke about the children, and never went by to see them. When I went over my mom's house she had company, her brother Benny, and my oldest sister Monica. I told them what the psychiatrist had gone over with me. "Monica, would you be the third signature?" "I don't know, Sis… I don't want to get involved with that nut." I assured my sister "Monica, it's going to be okay, he won't even know what is going on, and he doesn't even know what's going on around him now." I continued, "I was told by the doctor that many parents' have children with behavior problems. They don't know what to do to help them so they label the child with the word "bad," and send their child away to distant relatives in the hope they can do better for the child.

The child still has psychological problems, and they don't want to acknowledge what their child is doing." Monica spoke up, "Okay, maybe so, but what about the child? If the child is acting out as a cry for help, and no one answers, what then?"

My Uncle Benny stood up from his seat in the kitchen to speak to us in the living room. I could tell he had been drinking with my mom, "Then they turn out like Dennis; (The Pipe Man)." He overheard that Dennis was acting strange, so he added, "That guy is not acting. No! No! No! He is strange." He was saying this in a joking manner because you could tell he thought this was funny. "While he was in the pen, that was his name, and nobody ever forgot it." "We did time together, and one day this guard got him mad. Man! Dennis got a hold of a metal pipe, and wore out that guard. There were about ten guards on him but they were struggling with him, to control him. I don't think he even knew where he was, he was out of it. From that day on he's known as the "Pipe Man," and I'm telling you, didn't no one touch that guy or give him no shit. Girl that guy is crazy as hell."

None of this was made privy to me until now. After the marriage vows had been said or prior to the birth of my daughter, although I certainly would have her, even if alerted. As a matter of fact, after I was told about these episodes in his life, and I was also told, by my Uncle Benny, about all the other information he could remember about my husband. I was shocked, I felt deceived, and I felt let down by uncle.

"Let me see if I have this right. My uncle Benny, brother of my mother, spent time in prison during the same time my husband was incarcerated with him. This same uncle was around when I met my husband to be, and added his blessing when I announced that I was getting married. Uncle Benny, I had a child with this man. Did it ever occur to you to tell us this story before this? What in hell possessed you to believe it was okay to keep this information from me, your niece, and your blood?" Momma stepped up to correct my disrespectful language. "Watch your mouth, Sissy. You're still talking to your uncle." I replied angrily, "I'm not the one that has forgotten the blood… It seems to me that prison blood is more important than relative blood. Is that what I should believe Uncle Benny?" He tried to explain, and all I could tell was he realized he had put his foot in it, "Well baby, when you're in prison, what goes on there, will stay there." I knew you were with the guy, but how was I to know he didn't tell you? If I had told you, I really don't believe you would have believed me. You were in love." "I will never forgive you Uncle Benny, because now we will never know will we? All you had to do is make an effort... Try to talk to me. But that prison code was more important to you than my life."

I decided it was best to leave at this time before I said something really disrespectful. Monica had agreed to be the third signature in Dennis commitment hearing. I could tell my mother was getting nervous about how far this conversation was going to go. Upon my departure she had the final words; "I still say you need to come back home, and leave that fool alone. I keep having this dream about you trying to come home, but since that fool done cut off your legs, and arms, and you're rolling down the street crying in a small voice, help me, help me..."

The two weeks passed slowly. Dennis finally was involuntarily committed to an institution for the mentally ill, where he could get mental, and medical help. At twenty-five, I felt I was ill-prepared to handle it by myself, and although it hurt a lot to be without him, I knew it was best for him. I grieved for him like any other widow, but I felt cheated in some way. I was not given the noticed that most widows are given. If not a notice of illness or an accident; maybe even a body; they even have a funeral or ceremony of some sort. I was given nothing, nothing but an empty house, and two children to take care of. One day I just woke up, and my husband was no longer there. Instead, there lay the body of a strange man that was strange in more ways than one.

After Dennis' commitment hearing, I made every attempt to go on with my life. It was during this time I started modeling. I always wanted to be a model so I was allowed to take some classes after work with my mom's blessing, since she had to watch my children. I was no longer in dire need of cash, since I was now working as well as getting money through modeling jobs. With my life completely different these days, I discovered that it wasn't just the makeup that made me pretty.

I had friends that constantly told me how beautiful I was. People were now my friends for no other reason than to hear what I had to say. I didn't have to sell my body, or lie to men to get their money. I never told anyone about my past, but I was always afraid that one of my old tricks (men that I had sold my body to), would recognize me, and tell my friends. I wasn't interested in men at this time. Who had the time? My children kept me pretty busy outside of work, and modeling. My mom was really great about keeping them for me while I was working, but after she gave birth to twelve children herself; she was pretty adamant about not watching someone else's children. My life became a series of never ending nightmares which was actually a lot of hard work.

One that started with me getting up in the morning, dressing the children, dropping them off at my mother's house to catch the city bus; conscientiously reading the daily schedules to ensure I wasn't late to work. My job was tedious work indeed, punching out words on a computer keypunch machine. After work I would go to my mother's house to pick up the children, who by this time were hungry, and sleepy. After getting them home time together was a luxury which came in small bits that I valued, as much as, I valued my life. I had so little play time with them. I became dissatisfied with my life, as it was. It was in one of my many lonely nights that I heard my Lord's messages for my life. If one listens in total silence, a pin drop could be heard; this is when the Lord reveals himself to me.

Some people think the first word was the bible, but I believe the first word is his voice in your head. This is how the bible was written; this is Jesus' words. I believe some people don't realize the Lord didn't place us in this world to fail, but to prosper. People give too much credit to the devil. I don't. I do believe there is a devil, how can I believe in God, and not the other. But I believe it isn't the devil that makes something happen. Tribulations are just tests that the good Lord is taking us through; he needs to know if we're ready for the next step he has planned in our lives.

The Lord will never give us more than we can handle, so why wouldn't he give us a test. I knew that it was time for a change. I wasn't sure what I needed to do, but I knew it had something to do with the Army. I knew the day I was walking from the bus going to work. There was a recruiting poster in the window around the corner where

I worked so I walked into the building. I knew I was going to be late for work but I didn't care. I walked into the building, and stayed long enough to talk with a recruiter, and to fill out some paper work. When I got to my work station, I wasn't asked any questions so I didn't have to answer any questions. God is good. I really worried about how my parents would feel about this decision; so when I stopped by there to pick up the children, I asked my mother what she thought.

Road One or Two-Pick One; 1977

In 1977, Jimmy Carter succeeded Gerald Ford as the 39th President of the United States, U.S. President Jimmy Carter pardoned Vietnam War draft evaders, *"Roots[59]"* began its phenomenally successful run on ABC, the first *"Apple II[60]"* computers went on sale, the Supremes performed their final concert together at Drury Lane in London, England, and disbanded, *"Elvis Presley[61]"* performed his last concert, in Indianapolis, Indiana's Market Square Arena, *"David Berkowitz[62]"* was captured in Yonkers, New York, after over a year of murders in New York City as the Son Of Sam, *"Groucho Marx[63]"* died, the modern *"Food Stamp Program[64]"* began when the *"Food Stamp Act of 1977[65]"* was enacted, *"Reggie Jackson[66]"* blasted three home runs to lead the New York Yankees to a World Series victory over the Los Angeles, Dodgers.

It was also 1977 when Martin Luther King Junior's convicted killer, James Earl Ray, broke out of jail. He was caught three days later after a massive manhunt, *"Star Wars[67]"* opened at the cinema, and it was also when I approached my parents about leaving my children with them, while I joined the military. "There is no way in hell you're going to go off to the army, and I'm gonna be stuck with your children."

"But Momma, can't you see? This isn't about running away to get away from my children. It's about trying to do something to better their lives." I was twenty six when I explained to my parents, "I don't want to stay on welfare, or worse, continue to give my children those pennies rather than the dollars worth of happiness. I'm trying to give them a better life, but right now it's not going anywhere. If I don't do this, I don't know what else to do to give them more." I turned to my father,

"Daddy, please talk to Momma? Tell her what it's like to survive out there?" Daddy had once called me a "whore, and a tramp," because he knew what I had been doing with my life.

Even though he had not seen it with his own eyes, his friends would tell him. My Dad was always a man of few words, but when he said something it was final. "You go ahead, and join the army baby. Your Momma will be fine, she'll watch the kids. Just don't you worry about that?" I always believed I received my strength from my father; he was a strong, proud person, and I always hoped he had handed the trait down to me. He and my mother had twelve children together. We may not have had everything brand new; we may not have what everyone else had; but to tell you the truth, I never missed it until I was in high school, and someone told me I was supposed to have it. My mother was a Momma.

That said was enough, because they just don't make mothers like that, anymore. But my mother didn't have to prostitute to feed her children. She didn't have to steal, or shoplift, as it was called. She took care of the children, and Daddy took care of everything else. That is how I left to go into the military with my parents' blessing… at least one of them. I live for my children, and the military allowed me to take care of them in the way I felt they deserved. I needed more for my children.

The day I was to enter into the army I discovered a leftover of my previous lifestyle in my purse. It was a twenty cent (twenty dollars), bag of marijuana, which was from my going away party the night before. Here I was, sitting in the reception area of the hotel, with several other candidates, awaiting departure to a better life, and I had this marijuana in my possession. This is how I left my old lifestyle, and started my new lifestyle.

When I went to the bathroom, I looked in my purse staring at the twenty cent bag of marijuana. I was scared as hell. I had to get on a plane in less than a half hour, and I didn't know what to expect. I sure as hell didn't want to flush, or throw that entire bag of reefer down the toilet. But I also knew I wanted to succeed in this new life more than anything. I must have been crazy, because I stopped a girl I didn't even know. I told her, "Excuse me; I have a dilemma which I feel you could help me with. I have to get on that plane in a few minutes, but I just found this "twenty" in my purse from last night, but I can't just flush this much happiness down the drain." I continued, "If you want it, it's yours, free of charge."

She looked at me at first like I had lost my mind. I could tell she was wondering if I was trying to set her up. "I know what you're thinking, but I assure you this is no setup. I could get in trouble more than you for trafficking, or just having this stuff. I have had many days of pleasure with this stuff, which is why I can't flush it. Now if you don't want it, could you take it, and flush it for me; when I leave, of course?" We were both laughing by the time she made up her mind. Finally she made her decision. She grabbed the bag, and said, "What the hell." She grabbed the bag, turned, and ran out of the public bathroom. I just felt relieved.

I picked up my bags, and got on the plane. I didn't have any more contraband or marijuana until I completed my basic training that is, which lasted eight very long weeks. I remember first meeting Drill Sergeant Hartman. She was assigned to our platoon. "I'm your Platoon Sergeant. I will be the first person you answer to in the morning, and the last one you answer to at night. I will teach you how to be a soldier." "Whether we want you to, or not?" I whispered this in a low tone of voice to the soldiers around me. I said this partly because I have a personality that uses humor to cut tension. The other reason was because she looked like a woman that was tough, and probably liked women like the woman, named Nancy in my past. I didn't realize she had heard me. "Yes; whether you like it or not!"

With these last words, we were dismissed to go put our luggage away. I initially didn't like SGT Hartman. She was rude, rough, and heartless, as far as I was concern. I felt she was needlessly picking on me. No matter how hard I tried, it just wasn't good enough. I was a twenty six year old woman who had spent a lot of her time in taverns drinking or smoking marijuana, and cigarettes. Hell, the night I left for basic training, there was a big going away party. I don't even remember how I got to the airport. Now I had this mean ass drill sergeant that was going to do everything in her power to get me to fail.

I felt this way, at least seven of the eight weeks we were assigned to her. It just seemed like one day, it all just started to come together. Basic training was difficult, especially at first, but it was training that was healthy, and it raised my self-esteem. By the time I graduated from basic training, I felt all women should take it as a foundation to their adulthood. I truly felt every young woman should go through this program just to see what they were truly capable of. It made me so proud of myself; that I could run two miles, much less do it in record time.

I felt I achieved something great in my life when the drill sergeants told me I had passed the physical fitness test. When I ran the miles I wasn't so tired. Once you got your first wind you could continue forever. When I did the push-ups, I started to hold my head up higher. I actually shot expert at the M16A1 firing range. It was such a good feeling to graduate from basic training that I praised SGT Hartman for pushing us so hard. It was apparent that I was about to learn what I needed to maintain my adventure in a military lifestyle. Upon my arrival, I was tasked to carry my entire load of luggage, which I admit was a little much. Most of it was issued to me by the military. I soon learned the expression; "If you can't carry it, don't bring it." When I did arrive to my room, I realized the army truly believed in the buddy system. I had to share a room with another girl.

This was not the only thing I learned, as a newbie, which we new arrivals were called. I was placed with a group of people, which the military personnel called a Platoon. This group was determined by who was in either one building or another. The companies "Chain of Commands" was made up of one commander, a first sergeant, two or more platoon sergeants with a set of four groups each called squads, and the leaders were called squad leaders. The squads were composed of the privates, labeled private (PV1, PV2, PFC), from one to three and specialist (SPC, SPC 2 thru 5). A corporal was in charge of the squad. A person had to be appointed corporal. A corporal was a private with hard stripes.

This appointment is made if a higher ranking military leader identifies leadership characteristics in a person. I was a PV2 since my cousin came into the army with me. We didn't see much of each other, even though we were in the same brigade they put us in different buildings, which caused us to be in different platoons. I enjoyed being in my squad, mostly because I was sleeping with my squad leader. I was never given demerits nor did I really pay much attention to the cleaning parties (GI parties).

You're in the Army Now; 1978

It was 1978, when the *"Bee Gees[68]"* came out with: Night Fever, and Staying Alive, *"John Travolta[69],"* and *"Olivia Newton-John[70]"* was winning everyone's heart with: Grease, the *"Commodores[71]"* had everyone slow dancing to: Three Times a Lady, and I graduated from Advance Individual Training (AIT); I commenced onward to my first duty section in Germany.

One day prior to my departure my platoon sergeant called me into his office. I realized I was in trouble when I was told by my squad leader I had to report to our platoon sergeant. I would be telling a lie if I didn't say I wasn't scared. When I reported to the platoon sergeant in his office, I notice he wasn't smiling. I remember thinking that this must be serious.

Then he started off the conversation by asking me, "Are you married?" I thought, "If all he wanted was to check my records that was easy enough to do in the personnel office." But I said, "Yes Platoon Sergeant, technically." This was when he went into a long sermon about fornication. How it was a sin, and how what I was doing with his corporal was wrong because until I completed my marriage by getting a divorce, I should not be having sex with anyone else.

I felt that he had stepped well beyond his boundaries as a platoon sergeant; overstepping his area of responsibility for me by questioning my sex life. Since I really felt what we were doing was more like a game; all the marching, facing movements along with the physical fitness training, I didn't mind playing soldiers but I felt this was none of his business.

I asked him "Do you feel my actions as a soldier are less than your expectations? Am I not handling my duties as a soldier?" He said "The area of morality is a part of being a leader." He answered me with, "If you can't handle your self-control over your body, how could you; as a leader, set an example or counsel soldiers under your leadership." I was thinking the whole time he was lecturing me, that it was a shame he was such a stickler about sex, and God because he was really cute.

I explained to him "Yes, I realize it is a sin, Platoon Sergeant, but I had to put my husband in a mental hospital over a year and a half ago. I'm not ready to divorce him, nor do I plan to stay with the squad leader for life. I am merely having fun." I also indicated, "Now if you weren't my Platoon Sergeant, or so moralistic, and into right or wrong, I really had a slight crush on you sir. But if you want me to leave your corporal alone, I will, Platoon Sergeant." With that being said, and a salute, from me to him I asked him, "Am I excused, Platoon Sergeant." I think he was thrown off his guard, because all he said was "Carry on."

I'm sure now, as I look back on it; he felt I hadn't learned a thing, and that I wouldn't change my actions. In hindsight I believe that discussion made an impression on me in regard to my future actions and on my perception of life in general. I never forgot the things he said, and if I could find him now I would thank him from the bottom of my heart. With an about face, I left his office, and we never discussed it further. The rest of my time at my advanced individual training (AIT) was uneventful, until we received our orders to our first duty assignments.

I was given a two year tour to Germany. My cousin was being sent to Hawaii. She was happy that she was going to Hawaii. I didn't want to go that far from my children. If I had been assigned anywhere in the United States I would be able to bring my children with me. Since I was assigned to an overseas location, the children weren't allowed to go with me. I knew my mother would bust a gut when she found out.

Fortunately it wasn't as bad as I thought it would be. It seemed she was aware that it wasn't my fault. Prior to going to Germany I did get to visit my home state for thirty days prior to departing. When I arrived at my first active duty assignment I was like a sheep among a herd of cows. It was a small post, far from the command post. We worked for twelve hours on, and twelve hours off; if you were properly relieved by the oncoming shift. The only people you gain a relationship with are the ones you work with. There was also the grapevine which was abundant since gossip was immense in this small post.

I met this soldier named Larry, who loved to play chess. He was not in my unit, nor did I know any of his friends, at least to my knowledge. I don't even remember how we met but I stayed many hours in his room. It seems that the person I was assigned to live with was a lesbian, and I didn't want to be around her after she propositioned me. There was nothing but friendship, without benefits between Larry and me. As a matter of fact, I told Larry in detail of the day I was walking down the road; there were only dirt roads in this portion of Germany. "I glimpsed at this gorgeous man, while I was taking a walk to discover what this post had to offer." I said, "Hello." He said, "Hello."

Then we strolled on about our way. Nothing more took place, except my world took on another dimension. I fell hopelessly in love with this man. As I previously said, this was a small army post. I was scheduled to stay there for two years. If I knew anything about myself, I couldn't 'make love' with someone unless I thought I was 'in love' with that person; or at least in Lust. In my eyes, the only difference between love and lust is time.

One night, about three months after knowing Larry, I was in Larry's room drinking, talking and playing chess. Larry was, as usual, winning when his roommate walked in. All I could do was stand motionless at the stereo. Larry said to me laughingly, since his roommate was rushing over to his bed, "Sissy that was "T" (T stood for Taylor)." He grumbled something as he fell on his bed across the room. I didn't acknowledge his comment since I knew he didn't really want a reply. All he wanted was his bed which he flew toward it. I walked over to Larry. I had been telling Larry about this stranger I was in love with for about two months.

The time I said hello that first time, the times I ran into him since, and what little conversations we had. I didn't think Thomas had done anything harmful to cause me pain. I trusted him. Since I never told Thomas what T's name was, what he looked like or anything else he could have recognized about him. All I could say was, "That is him." Larry said, "He, who?" I whispered, "The man I've been telling you about, dummy. I have to go, really." I started for the door. We had been drinking quite a bit so Larry said, "Sissy, stop; let me walk you to your room." I said quickly, "That won't be necessary. I'll see you tomorrow." I bolted from the room.

The next day I was scheduled to work after eight in the morning so I arose, and got dressed to go running. After my run, I stopped over Larry's room, and he answered the door. I asked him, "Are you alone?" I had never asked him this before. I would just assume he was alone. It was at this time he said, "Yeah, of course, T's working." I asked him, "How could this have happened." He said, "I'm not sure, except for the fact that I rarely see him." He said, "I work in another field than you guys do since my field is so rare, I'm the only one stationed here." I asked him, "What field is he in?" He answered, "He's a 72E. He's also usually over in his girlfriend's room when he's not working. Sissy, you can't believe I had anything to do with this mess." He sounded so hurt, and confused. I could understand his need to protect our friendship since I also felt a need to maintain this friendship. I said, "Larry, no, never. I don't believe you had any involvement in this mess. I am just trying to figure this out."

I continued, "You say he's a 72E, which is what I am. I don't know everyone in my section. I just know the ones on my shift. He has a girlfriend that he cares a lot about, which explains his whereabouts after duty hours." Larry interrupted me with, "His girlfriend is pregnant. People call her Lil' Bit because she is so small, maybe about five feet. He stands over six feet, two inches," and he is so devoted to her, and they look so cute together. He told me last night they got into a disagreement, which is why he got drunk, and returned to his room so late." I was startled to hear that his lady friend was pregnant. I figured that meant he was off the market. He was still the cutest man on this small ass military post. "I believe he may work in the telecommunication center (TCC), with me but on another shift." Larry agreed with me so we went on to another subject. He was just glad to know that I didn't blame him.

White Men Can Jump

A few days later I was changed to another shift which was when I was formally introduced to Specialist (SPC) Anthony Taylor. It seemed a shame for someone as tall as he was to be wasted on such a short person. Although I still felt he was gorgeous, there was an even greater reason for me not to venture into a relationship with him. He outranked me in our chain of command so he knew that if he approached me he could get into a lot of trouble. Our shift consisted of two people on duty for twelve hours. I believe he was trying to get me to hate him. As he slept throughout the shift, he had me mopping, and buffing the TCC floor. When it was shift change he would wake up, and act like he did all the work to the oncoming shift.

Although I wasn't too happy with SPC Taylor, I still felt a real closeness to Lil' Bit once I met her. She was everything Larry had said she was. We would talk for hours about little or nothing. It just so happened, that she went into labor, and she couldn't find SPC Taylor anywhere. When she knocked on my door, I didn't hesitate to take her to the next town, where the hospital was located. I had a privately owned vehicle (POV), which wasn't something everyone had. Once she had the baby I went back to our little government post, picked up SPC Taylor, and took him to see his son at the hospital. They told me I was the baby's godmother, but I never saw them again.

When they offered me a position in another TCC, which was miles away, I immediately took it. It just wasn't healthy being in love with someone that didn't love you back. Especially, when you valued the friendship with the other woman, for these reasons I determined it was time to get away.

Something I should have learned, but didn't, until my second assignment on my first tour of duty. I learned to never mix business with pleasure. I learned this lesson when I was reassignment in Germany to the main headquarters within another military post in Germany. I didn't apply it when I had an affair with my senior sergeant; he was the senior non-commissioned officer in charge (SNCOIC). It started off so innocently. He was a very humorous individual that got along with everyone. I respected him in every way. I was a workaholic so much of my life; it was understandable that I spent so much of my tour in the Telecommunication Center I was assigned to. The one thing that drew us together was working hard, and staying long hours at work together in the effort to get the work load lowered.

One day, he and I were the only two left at work. There usually are at least six of us, but for some reason unbeknownst to me, the schedule had only four people on duty, and two people had to go home prior to the end of our shift. Sergeant Escobar was the scheduling sergeant. I felt that he arranged this schedule merely because he knew that between the two of us, we could get the work done, as well as, another priority while I was too dim-witted to see.

Although I didn't want to believe that he had premeditated this arrangement to get at me, but I did think it, but it was too late by the time I considered it. He was also known as the most congenial noncommissioned officers (NCO) of all of the other assigned NCOs. We finally got to the end of the shift. We had worked fourteen hours of a twelve hour shift. It was raining outside, and he had a car. After we finally got released by the oncoming shift Staff Sergeant Escobar asked me if I wanted a ride home.

Since I was married, and had dependants (my two children), the army regulations allowed me to stay off post. I couldn't bring them with me, but I could get housing. Maybe it was because a raid could happen at any time in this area. I told him I would love a ride home. We had both worked so hard we were pretty tired. Once we arrived at my apartment, I asked him if he wanted to see the inside of my apartment. We were in Germany, and the homes were quite different from the states. He agreed to go up to my place. We had been laughing all day, since he had an ability to brighten up the room.

As I gave him a drink, we talked some more. "So Sarge, are you married?" He answered, "Yes, I have three daughters. We agreed that it would be better if I came on this assignment alone. That way I would return in two years instead of three. What about you? What's your situation?" "I'm still married, but I had him committed to a mental institution. I have two children, and that's all I think about. I can't wait to get back to them. I thought I was going to be with them after my Advanced Initial Training (AIT), but I got assigned here in Germany. This is an unaccompanied tour of duty.

I guess I will have to wait until I get back to the states." He asked me with a twinkle in his eyes, "Do you get lonely? I know I do." I answered, "Of course I do. I just keep working, and thinking of my children. I find it makes the time go by. What do you do to make the time go by?" He got up, and walked over to my chair, sitting closer to me. "You are such a pretty girl; also smart, and I like that." "Sarge, what has that got to do with what I just asked you?" He answered, "That's because I'm getting bored with the small talk. All I really want to do is kiss you." "What about your wife?"

Sergeant Escobar placed his hand on my arm, just below the sleeve. He was touching my skin. He asked me, "Have you ever made it with a white man?" I told him I had not, and I continued, "It really doesn't matter to me whether a person is white or black. It would probably matter if they were purple or green." I was trying to inject a little humor into the situation. I have to admit I was getting a little more than anxious by now.

I think people are all the same inside. I continued, as I began to walk around the room we were in. "That is what is important, what's inside. Have you made it with a black girl before?" He was slowly following me, and by now he was very close to me, and I could feel the heat rising between my legs. I tingled at the place where his hands were. It had been such a long time since I had been touched like this, and I did wonder if any of the stories about white boys were true.

He asked me, "Do you believe what they say about white men having a small penis?" He startled me since it was like he was reading my mind. I laughed when I said, "If I believed that I would have to believe black men have tails." Half the laughter was because I said this. I was silently thinking of what he asked me, and the other nervous laughter was because I actually wanted him to continue, and I so hoped what the people said about white men was not true. Sergeant Escobar asked, "Aren't you curious? Not even a little bit." He asked this as he skillfully placed his hand under my t-shirt.

We still had our uniforms on, but it didn't look like we would have them on much longer. I said in a laughing manner, "Sarge (This was a version of endearment of the word sergeant, used only if given permission to do so.), what are you doing? Are you aware that you're married, and you are my supervisor?" By now he was kissing me on my neck as he continued to rub my back underneath my shirt. "So you ask me all this because you are planning to turn me in? Do you want me to stop? That should be the only question you should be asking yourself about now. Do you want me to go away?"

He definitely knew what he was doing with his hands, with his body, and with my mind. He placed my hand in his pants, where I felt his manhood. The story circulated about white men was definitely not true about him. I felt weak, and hot all over. The only thing I could think of was how quickly I could get my pants off so I could feel his manhood touching me. I just wanted him inside of me. As he slowly removed my panties I knew he was toying with me. I knew by the width, and length of his penis, and our labored breathing that he wanted it as much if not more than I did.

We both still had our boots on, and our pants only went down to our feet as I turned around, allowing him to enter me from behind. His manhood was hot, and satisfying. It was so good, all I could think was "I think I love you." I knew this was ridiculous since neither of us said anything about love. I was beginning to believe my ideal of love was the satisfaction I felt after my lust. I knew this, at least on his part, was nothing more than lust. He was fun to be with, he was a workaholic like me, and he knew what he was doing in the bedroom. It seemed like that's all that was necessary.

Lessons Learned; 1979

During 1979, the U.S., and the *"People's Republic of China*[72]*"* established full diplomatic relations, convicted bank robber, *"Patty Hearst*[73]*"* was released from prison after her sentence was commuted by U.S. President Jimmy Carter, in a ceremony at the White House, *"President Anwar Sadat of Egypt,*[74]*"* and *"Prime Minister Menachem Begin of Israel*[75]*"* signed a peace treaty. The *"Iraqi President Hasan al-Bakr*[76]*"* resigned, and *"Vice President Saddam Hussein,*[77]*"* replaced him. A major *"gay rights*[78]*"* march in the U.S. took place in Washington, D.C., involving many tens of thousands of people, *"U.S. Senator Edward Moore Kennedy*[79]*"* announced that he would challenge President Jimmy Carter for the 1980 Democratic Presidential Nomination, in response to the hostage situation in *"Tehran,*[80]*"* U.S. President Jimmy Carter ordered a halt to all oil imports into the U.S. from Iran, U.S. President Jimmy Carter issued *"Executive Order 12170,*[81]*"* freezing all *"Iranian*[82]*"* assets in the U.S., and U.S. banks in response to the hostage crisis, at which time Iranian leader *"Ruhollah Khomeini*[83]*"* ordered the release of thirteen female, and African American hostages being held at the U.S. Embassy in Tehran and I discovered white men can jump.

In Kaiserslautern, Germany, Sergeant Escobar and I continued to see each other in this manner for at least six months. We would work, very hard, and then after we completed our shift we would go back to my apartment to work even harder. I called it having sex since that is all it really was, no matter how good it was. He was white, but that didn't bother me. He was also married, which did bother me, but not enough to let him go. By the time six months had passed I thought I loved him, but I found out that he was just having another affair on his wife.

He approached me; I normally would never have thought of being romantically involved with a white man. I had failed to see through his façade. Somehow I had convinced myself if I made sex good enough; he would divorce his wife, and marry me. He made it perfectly clear that it was lust between us. Our relationship ended abruptly when a new black girl arrived to Germany. I looked a lot better than her, at least to me, but I guess he wasn't looking at the face. She was assigned to our unit, and the next thing I knew, he was being seen with her everywhere. I, for the second time in my life, felt jealousy.

Every time I saw them together… that green monster would creep within my whole being to look at them so happy. This was me two weeks ago, and I didn't know what I did to make him turn on me this way. I finally caught him in a private setting, and decided that it was time for a showdown. I asked him, "What happened? Did I do anything wrong?" Sergeant Escobar smiled with that beautiful boyish face. He didn't touch me or anything, but I felt like he had punched me in the gut when he said, smiling, "You didn't do anything wrong, it's just over. I'm with Michelle now."

I couldn't help the emotions that I felt. The feelings were pulled together in a knot in the pit of my stomach. I loved this man, yet he is treating me like the garbage you would throw out. I now had to work with not only him, but also the girl that he was now seeing. I could have brought him up on charges, since he was my senior. He was a supervising sergeant in charge of the shift I worked in, and I was a subordinate. Sergeant Escobar was married, and adultery was also a charge punishable in the army under the *"Uniform Code of Military Justice (UCMJ),[84]."* I did none of the above. I felt I knew all this when I stated this relationship, and no matter how deep the knife was in my back I couldn't lower myself by doing something so harmful to retaliate. I struggled through my days at work, holding my chin up.

When I returned to my home, I would cry myself to sleep, realizing how big a fool I was to fall for this loser. When you are in charge, I discovered, you owe more to the people than they owe to you. I once again remembered my old platoon sergeant in AIT, and his words. Once the colonel of the brigade I was a part of, was deployed to the field to complete a communication exercise. Our company took pride in going out, and performing our duties well. That meant in order for us to successfully communicate, it had to be done in a timely manner. There was another company in the brigade that had no desire to be out there in the snow, and cold. They had a bad attitude, and didn't care who knew it. We were out there for three days trying to communicate within this battalion. Soon the word got back to the colonel that this company had coined the phrase, "We can't communicate, and you can't make us." Well, our company was released, along with two other companies were told to go back to the rear. The exercise was over for us, but for the other company, it had only begun.

They got to stay up front with the colonel, and I dare say, he made them communicate before they returned. Three weeks later, they were some communicating soldiers. Although he had to stay out there with them, he proved to them that they could, and would communicate. They discovered within themselves a sense of purpose, and fulfillment. As the saying goes, "It's not about the destination, it's about the journey." This is one incident which I reminisce about the good days of my military life, one that demonstrates the cohesiveness of soldiers. There are also the incidents where it goes without saying that people can be so back stabbing, vindictive, and selfish in the military.

I remember getting up one night in the field. It was time for the shift change in the van atop the hill in a five ton truck. Being in the field with the military was never scary to me because we knew the military would take care of us. But this field duty we parked the vans in one area and pitched our tents in another location. It was walking distance, but when you wake up at midnight and start walking alone in a field it gets kind of scary. I started walking and whistling, and it seemed the farther I walked, the scarier it got.

It wasn't too long before I started hearing repeated baaing in the background. It was so cloudy I couldn't see five feet in front of me. The sound of sheep increased, and it seemed the farther I walked the closer the sounds were. I have to be honest; I was about to turn around because I was beginning to have visions of being the victim of a stampede. I knew I was a non-commissioned officer (NCO) and was needed in my van with the soldiers that worked with me; but I don't think the sheep cared about my rank.

On the other hand I was a city girl that had never seen sheep except on television, especially up close, and in numbers. Suddenly I heard the sound of someone else in the field with me. I heard the sound of someone else whistling besides myself. I laughingly yelled out, "Who goes there?" I heard the voice of a man that sounded just as relieved as I was, "Private Chambers mame," It's amazing how relaxed one can be as long as there is someone else in danger with you. There were a lot of sheep out there but there was a very thin fence made of rope that was the equivalent of a fence of yarn, which is why we couldn't see it. This was set out there to keep them in the right area. Since it was snowing and dark we couldn't see it but the sheep could. We were never in any danger, but in the middle of the night, alone, we didn't know that. Once we were a set, we were no longer afraid.

Actually, we thought, as we continued on our journey to our duty sections, our fear was funny, and ridiculous. One field training exercise began with the lower enlisted soldiers setting up three, general purpose, "GP medium[85]" tents; two for the senior enlisted soldiers, one for the males and the other for the females, and one GP medium tent for the field chow hall. "Pup tents[86]" were constructed with two pieces of water proof tenting material for the lower enlisted soldiers. Each lower enlisted soldier carried as part of their field gear one piece of this material. The lower enlisted soldiers were to pair up and sleep in their pup tents which were just large enough to house two bodies.

After the field site was constructed the pot bellied stoves were being fired up to heat up the GP medium tents. The other noncommissioned officers (NCOs) were having a hard time getting the stoves to operate so I volunteered to light it. What I did not know was that someone had put diesel fuel in the cans marked "Mogas.[87]" Mogas burns at a lower temperature than "diesel fuel[88]," which we used to fuel the military vehicles. I took the fuel can, and poured it into the stove. When the match was applied to the fuel, there was a tall funnel cloud that spread over the ceiling, inside the tent.

As the other soldiers ran out of the tent all I could do was stand there next to the stove with my mouth wide open. I remember thinking, "Wow. How pretty those flames are." I'm not even sure who it was but someone grabbed my arm, and pulled me out of the tent before it was engulfed by the flames. I was an experienced soldier that had operated field stoves prior to this incident. I was also not held responsible for the tent; which was totally burned down. Upon the graduation of this class I was awarded a bright red entrenching tool (shovel), which all of the graduating class had signed? It was a joke but I valued not only the bright red shovel, but all the signatures more.

Drugs!!! Who Me

My assignment in Germany was very different from what I expected. I did get assigned to a unit where I could actually use the vocation I was trained to do. It was great being in a unit that accomplished so much. What I was surprised at was the drugs that were so readily available. I remembered when I first met my roommate. She started to light a pipe that was filled with hashish. Of course she was checking me out, but she soon realized I had only one issue about her getting high; she was doing it without me.

I was just making a determination as to whether it was a safe drug since I never heard of hashish, and how fast I could get high. Since I was not privy to hash in the states, I asked her questions about what it was. It seemed that marijuana was not easy to attain in Germany, and once it arrived, it really wasn't that good. I soon was a member of the group of people that got high on hashish in their rooms on a daily basis. I was also introduced to a dietary product called *"X1-12,*[89]*"* which was also banned by the military.

It was sold over the counter, on the economy (A term coined by the military for the German areas not encompassed by the military post). Yes, I and a number of other soldiers, abused the drug, or maybe we abused ourselves depending on how you felt when you came down. X1-12 was great to used after partying, and getting drunk all night or just to stay up to party. It allowed me to drink all night, and never get drunk. Hashish, and X1-12 was the party drugs of Germany. I used X1-12 daily but if the military would have had the urinalysis test the military has today; we would not have been able to use it. The checks and balances of the Food and Drug Administration (FDA) that we have in the U.S. are not as lenient as it is overseas. I felt that taking hashish, and X1-12 didn't seem to be bad on the body. Looking back on this, I probably could get a doctorate as a doctor for all the drugs I confidently administered, and pronounced "was or wasn't" good for me, and others.

After completing a tour in (Germany I was given orders to go back to the states. I was assigned to MacDill AFB for three years) I was allowed to take my family with me. My life seemed so different from the one I had in Milwaukee. The people were different in such a way that everyone had a job and were looking forward to their future lives. The environment was definitely different, but not so deep inside that I wasn't the same girl inside. I would go to the NCO Club, and meet men. If I liked them, I would sleep with them. I thought I was so unique by treating the men in the same fashion they had treated me, prior to my enlistment. I had worth now, and I wasn't about to let just anyone into my life. If they needed a place to stay, they would have to go elsewhere to find it. This stop over was just that, "Stop, than get over it." I only had room enough, in my heart, for the love I carried for my children. The one thought I had at night, and the first thing I thought about in the morning. "How can I get my children back?" I knew I could bring them to Georgia. But first I had to fight the institution.

Being sent to Macdill Air Force Base in Tampa Florida when I left Germany. Upon my arrival, I was directed to the location of the building that housed the enlisted personnel, which is where the reception soldiers directed me. Once inside of my room I felt relief from the way I felt outside of the room. Outside I could actually feel all the eyes on me.

I was putting my bags away when I heard some noise out in the front of my window. When I looked out of the window, there were three females out pulling up something. I heard them talking, "That new girl has probably been placed here to catch us. She seems as if they put her here from the Criminal Investigation Department (CID). She looks older than us soldiers. The CID takes us for stupid." I thought it was so funny that these soldiers thought I was CID. I said in a low voice, but loud enough for them to hear me… "I'm not CID, and I can prove it by smoking one now… I could truly use one. It's a shame how marijuana makes you paranoid." They looked at me embarrassed, than it turned into humor. We all got a good laugh later, as we smoked a joint, and told old stories about our adventures.

It was at this assignment that I was taken to meet my non-commissioned officer in charge (NCOIC) on a motorcycle. I had never ridden on a motorcycle, and it was scary. The soldier didn't give me much of a choice when she pulled up to me, she said, "Get on." With me in my uniform;, we road on the interstate. I was so surprised that when we arrived at our destination it was on a beach. The ocean was so beautiful, and I don't think I will ever forget the black van that was parked on the white sand. I felt the sand give way under the black boots that I was wearing. As I approached the door of the van, I felt unsure as to whether I wanted to knock on the door or not.

I pushed the chill away, and knocked only to face the open door, and the strong smell of marijuana as it escaped the van. There was an overweight black man who was perched in his seat in a compartment of the van that had been decorated in such dark colors to make it resembled an apartment or some get high room which I had been in before. The people inside wasn't in uniform, and I remembered thinking how overweight he was so could he even get in a uniform. He said, "I'm Sergeant Blakely, I am your section chief, and this is my place of employment. If you need anything, or something comes up, you can't handle, just call one of the section leaders, and they will direct the information to me. Your duty assignment is for six months here at Macdill Air Force Base, and six months duty out on any desert in the world.

That being said you can be two weeks here, four weeks somewhere else. You will not spend more than a month in any location. When you are here your job is to get ready for the next destination. Any questions? Have a joint?" He said this with such a manner of normalcy that I really didn't know whether it was me that was normal or not. I did decide that there was no way in hell I could stay here in this beautiful location. I couldn't get my children to this location, not knowing when I was leaving or when I'd return, much less being around this place that is profuse with marijuana.

I had to get a deferment of my duty assignment. It didn't take long to get my deferment since they knew I had two children, and I knew my section chief's little secret. I did not go back to the van, ever. When the order came in, I was one happy girl. I just knew I was about to get my children back with me. I soon discovered it wasn't going to be as easy as I thought. I was reassigned from Tampa, Florida, to Augusta, Georgia. I soon worked with a unit that trained the soldiers in a simulated outdoor environment.

There were vans lined up in a training situation that was repetitive to say the least. The young soldiers that came through didn't realize that even the jokes were repeated. The good thing was the fact that my children could be with me after work. It was circulating around the grape vine that the military could, with the use of a test called a urinalysis, find out whether marijuana or other drugs were in your system. It was supposed to be accurate for up to forty-five days after use. I had some hard decisions to make. Now I know I have already mentioned how I loved smoking marijuana.

It was now time for me to decide whether I wanted to take the consequences of smoking bad enough to get caught by the military police. I had achieved the rank of SGT (E5), so it was a decision that needed to be addressed. Did I enjoy smoking marijuana enough to chance the consequence of losing my rank, as well as the loss of my career with the military, and maybe even military prison? The military had decided they were seeking a no tolerance stand, when it came to drugs. They were actually putting soldiers out of the military if caught using drugs. That was if they were lucky enough not to spend time in Leavenworth (this being a military prison). This new test was not only getting praise from the top military ranks, the respect for it was obvious by the number of soldiers being put out. The choice was simple; if I smoked marijuana, I would lose my career, if I lost my career, I couldn't smoke marijuana anyway since I would have no money.

My decision was to stop smoking marijuana or take any drug. Little did I realize that I would substitute the marijuana use to the legal drug; alcohol. I had finally gotten a trailer where we could reside. Thomas and Dee were in school during the day so it wasn't a problem that I worked all day. By this time Thomas was nine and Dee was five; we had great times together. Thomas was really helpful when it came to babysitting Dee, and helping around the house.

I still remember when Thomas found the pond behind the trailer park. He would disappear for hours. Once I had gotten them a kitten, which seemed like a good ideal at the time. When we got home one day to find the kitten had gotten into some kind of trouble because it had a broken leg. It had been in the trailer all day so it had to be that it did it to itself. The veterinarian said, after putting a cast on its leg, that it would take about four to six weeks to heal.

Life's Deceptions; 1980

It was 1980 when U.S. President Jimmy Carter announced the U.S. would boycott the *"1980 Summer Olympics in Moscow,[90]" "Archbishop Oscar Romero[91]"* was killed by gunmen while celebrating mass in *"San Salvador,[92]"* and at his funeral six days later, forty-two people were killed amid gunfire, and bombs. The U.S. severed diplomatic relations with Iran, and imposed economic sanctions, following the taking of American hostages on November 4, 1979, *"Operation Eagle Claw,[93]"* a commando mission in Iran to rescue American embassy hostages, was aborted after mechanical problems grounded the rescue helicopters, and eight U.S. troops were killed in a mid-air collision during the failed operation.

A Miami, Florida court acquitted four white police officers of killing *"Arthur McDuffie,[94]"* a black insurance executive, provoking three days of race riots, the *"Star Wars Episode V: The Empire Strikes Back[95]"* is released *"Pac-Man[96]"* (the best-selling *"arcade game"* of all time) was released, the *"Cable News Network (CNN)[97]"* is officially launched, in Los Angeles, comedian *"Richard Pryor"* was badly burned trying to freebase cocaine, the *"African National Congress[98]"* in South Africa published a statement by their imprisoned leader, *"Nelson Mandela,[99]"* U.S. President Jimmy Carter signed *"Proclamation 4771,[100]"* requiring eight-teen to twenty-five year old males to register for a peacetime *"military draft,[101]"* in response to the *"Soviet invasion of Afghanistan,[102]"* U.S. President Jimmy Carter defeated Senator Edward Kennedy to win re-nomination, at the *"1980 Democratic National Convention[103]"* in New York City, and *"U.S. Presidential Election, 1980.[104]"*

1980 witnessed Republican challenger and former Governor Ronald Reagan of California defeat incumbent Democratic President Jimmy Carter, exactly one year after the beginning of the *"Iran hostage crisis.*[105]*"* A record number of viewers (for an entertainment program) tuned into the *"U.S. TV soap opera Dallas*[106]*"* to learn who shot lead character J.R. Ewing, the Who shot J.R.? event was an international obsession, and although I initiated my divorce from my first husband in 1979, I received my divorce from Dennis in 1980. Although the world was busy creating life changing history, I was busy trying to get our cat out of a tree.

Several days earlier, the three of us had selected a kitten from a woman giving the cats away. The price was right, and the children had many hours of amusement with this kitten. One day we returned to our trailer from the school I picked up the children from when I left my duty station for the day. Upon entering our trailer, we found the kitten somehow had broken his leg. We took him to the veterinarian who put a cast on the kitten. After the cast came off, the cat's leg was repaired, and he started to play with the children again. A couple of days later, after I arose to start my new day, I couldn't find the kitten in the trailer.

I stepped outside, and I heard a meow. That is when I found the cat up in a tall pine tree. I tried to get it to come down, but the more I tried the higher it went. I called our veterinarian who only explained that since the cat previously had a bad fracture, he wouldn't trust climbing out of the tree. The next day I called the fire department to ask them what I should do. They sent some firemen over to assist me. "Unfortunately..." they explained, "...if you wait five or six days the cat will come down, but it wouldn't be alive."

I left for work telling them "Shoot it down and take it away." I said this while turning around to enter into my trailer. I still needed to get dressed into my uniform so I could go to work. I fully understood what they meant. I couldn't have my children traumatized by their cat, lying on the ground when they got home from school. At least if they shot the cat down it would be a controlled situation. When they asked me where the cat was, I told them the cat found his own family, and moved away.

Our quarters (military housing), finally became available so we moved on post. Unfortunately what I didn't realize was the fact that the gain of on-post housing would cause us a loss of the quarter's allotment on my paycheck. It was a pretty hefty piece of lost cash. When I had the trailer it was okay, because the trailer didn't cost that much. I wish I had done the math prior to accepting the quarters and allowing the military to move us. That allowance (money) would not be available to us anymore.

It became apparent that I was sinking fast, financially. It would have been okay except I realized that I couldn't feed my children. I would have gotten another job, but my commander wouldn't allow me too, which was the regulation in the army. It was breaking my heart, but I realized that I had to send them back to my mother. Once I realized what I was doing for them was best for them I made arrangements to send them back to my mother. I knew that if I couldn't feed them it was bad for them.

If I didn't pay the bills, the army would send them back and demote me. They would take away the rank I fought so hard to get, which was not going to fix my financial problems. This was the army's solution for not taking care of your family or your finances, the military Uniform Code of Military Justice (UCMJ). I called my brother in Milwaukee and paid for him to travel from Milwaukee to travel to Georgia; he would go with them back to Milwaukee. It was years later that he informed me how irresponsible he was.

While he was taking them back he had left them in the bus station waiting area, to wait for him. So he could go have a beer across the street. While he was at that club, the place got raided, a fight broke out, and he almost was taken to jail. Thomas was nine, Dee was six, and they were waiting in the bus station alone. I am so glad I didn't find out about it until they were grown. It took a few years for me to get pass the pain of losing them. I spent most of my free time in my on post room, out on the town, or around the barracks; all of which were spent drinking a lot. I gave up my quarters, since I didn't have my children around; I sent the money to my mother again. She, I'm sure, needed it. It took a promotion to Staff Sergeant (SSG/E6), before I tried living in an apartment again.

I had a brief affair with my Brigade Command Sergeant Major (CSM). He wasn't fat, the army wouldn't stand for that, but he was close to it. I didn't love him. He was useful in regards to getting into the

Officers Club, and staying out of trouble. When some supervisor decided I wasn't doing what I was told, I could go to him, and manipulate him to get what I wanted. I had gotten dissatisfied with my life. The whole reason I was struggling with this military life was to get close to my children, and to give them a better life. It still wasn't happening. I was frustrated with my life, and it just seemed like no matter what I did the whole purpose for my life was gone. I had sex with the CSM, I got involved with a female soldier, and I also was having sex with the Supply Officer (O2). I believe he was younger than I but he was built.

I would go to his office, and have sex right on his desk, while his soldiers were working for him outside of the door. I thought this was a thrill, and very risky. The sex wasn't bad either. There was also a Captain (O1), in charge of a company. He would take me out to eat, and we would meet in his off post apartment for sex. I realize that all of these relationships were not for love or even for a lasting relationship. Need I say I was drinking a lot during this time in my life?

Why did I have sex with the female soldier? I don't know or care. I was pretty much staying in my room alone, a lot. Since I sent my children home I was doing a lot of drinking in my room alone. She lived in my barracks. One day I answered the knock on my door, and it was her. "Hey, what do you need?" She answered, "You. I've been watching this door since you got here, and I thought we could get along." I said, "If you've been watching this door, you probably noticed I don't want to be bothered." She returned, "No, I don't think that is the conclusion I came up with. I figured you've had a hard time, and like me, maybe you just need a friend to talk to. I like your style."

By now I had moved away from the door, and she stepped into my room, as I went to my drink, which I had already poured before she knocked on the door. She was saying, "I've had a pretty bad experience here in the military myself. I'm tired of these guys taking advantage of me than going to the next girl. All I want is a little companionship with no strings attached, but they just don't get it." I told her, "You ought to do what I do, which is living for me, no matter how they feel. You need to thicken your skin, and start using them instead of putting yourself in a position to get hurt."

She moved closer to me, and asked, "Have you ever been with a girl? You know sexually." I could not understand why females always ask that question. "What different does it make? Either I want to have sex with you or I don't. Why, are you trying to get with me?" She answered, "Well you don't have to be so mean about it. I was just trying to see if you were willing to have a relationship with me." I asked her, "Why didn't you just say that when you knocked on the door? You are just as bad as the men you say hurt you. You came in this room specifically trying to be with me, but then you talk all this shit instead of coming to the point. You want to be my friend?" I said this last sentence sarcastically.

I was not in the mood to get bamboozled by this woman so I asked, "Instead of asking me about my pass discretions, show me what you've got to offer." She leaned over to kiss me, and I turned my head, "Wrong. Go lower..." She got on her knees, and pulled my panties off. I let her without participating or showing much concern. She placed her hands on my thighs, and started to lick tenderly. It really felt pretty good. I backed up, and lay on the bed so she could get her tongue on my pussy. Of course this wasn't the first time I opened my legs, and had someone, male or female, service me down there but it was the first time I acted like it didn't matter to me. It gave me a sense of power.

I'm pretty sure I liked the power more than I enjoyed the act. This woman had come to my room to find out if she could get with me, as she put it, but she couldn't just be honest. How dare her, coming in here with the bull about wanting to be friends. She talks about men using her with their lies, but she had the nerve to try me. Even if she wasn't very smart, she still could have come to me correctly. I didn't want to be her friend, and I wasn't going to service her.

I don't know where or who was in her pussy last. I allowed her to service me while I told her where to put her tongue, how to touch my body. But I was not going to service her back. She deserved whatever I did to her as I slapped her on her ass, while telling her what to do. After I had an orgasm, I told her, "I'm not going to do it to you since I don't know you, but we can remain friends. If you need to be with me again you're welcome to knock on my door. You're pretty good with that tongue of yours, but I bet you already knew that." She blushed as she answered, "Yeah, I've been told." I said, "See, that's what I'm talking about. No telling who's been with you."

She was asking for my approval as she stood next to me as I pulled my clothes together. "You don't have to do me. I get off just pleasing you. Was it really good for you?" "Yeah it was alright. You do know that you are your own worst enemy, right? You say you are tired of men taking you for granted and yet you come in here, and allow me to use you than put you out. You don't know me from Adam (with a smile on my face), or should I say Eve? Is it so much better to be messed over by a woman?"

She looked sad, "I took a chance. I saw you, and I thought you would be good. I don't know much about you but I do know you got some good pussy." She said this with a laugh. I just looked at the ceiling when I said, "Girl you are one sick puppy. There is no helping you. By the way, what is your name and which door is yours?" "Oh I thought I told you, my name is Roxanne, and I stay over there." She said with a laugh. I looked at her with a smile, and told her, "Roxanne, go home." I saw her again about three more times when she made the mistake of telling me she loved me. That was when she had to go.

I didn't mind her servicing me, but I didn't want to be in a monogamist relationship with a woman. I loved men too much to let anyone know I was being with a woman. "Alright, now you've done it. You just ended this good thing. I am not about to love you, and you are not going to make me feel guilty. Remember you approached me, and said you wanted no strings attached." She looked at me with tears in her eyes, "Please don't stop seeing me. I won't hold you to strings. I can't help it how I feel. I was just telling you because I do love you, but you don't have to love me back. Please don't make me go."

I remembered being in her shoes, and it hurt so much when you love someone whom you'll do anything to keep seeing, (Kevin). I felt sorry for her. I shouldn't have but I did. "You know, regardless of what you say, it is going to hurt you to continue in this relationship because I can't, or won't return the feelings. I'm not there in my life. I don't want to feel emotions for anyone right now. You need to go, and don't come back. Respect me for being honest with you, and find someone that can return your love. You're a nice enough woman, Roxy you're just sick. You need help." She turned, and walked away, and that was the last time we were alone with each other anyway.

Young Love; 1981

It was 1981; *"Ronald Reagan[107]"* succeeded Jimmy Carter, as the *"fortieth President of the U.S.,[108]"* minutes later, Iran released the *"fifty-two Americans[109]"* held for four hundred, and forty-four days, ending the Iran Hostage Crisis, CBS Evening News' *"Walter Cronkite[110]"* signed off for the last time, the *"Centers for Disease Control and Prevention[111]"* reported that five homosexual men in Los Angeles, California had a rare form of pneumonia seen only in patients with *"weakened-immune systems[112]"* (the first recognized cases of "AIDS"), *"Wayne Williams,*113" a twenty-three year old African American, was arrested and charged with the murders of two other African Americans. He is later accused of twenty-eight others, in the Atlanta Child Murders, *"Simon & Garfunkel[114]"* performed the *"Concert in Central Park,[115]"* a free concert in New York, in front of approximately half a million people, and I met Tony.

I met Tony after I was assigned as an instructor in the building we both worked in, I was introduced to him. I wasn't looking for any relationship. I was tired of people, and their games. Since that episode in Germany, I had a pretty solid hold on never getting involved with anyone I worked around again. I would walk down the hall, in the building I worked in. It never dawned on me that I could get involved with someone in the same building I worked in.

It never dawn on me that the individual I spoke to daily would soon play such a dominate role in my life. As a matter of fact the gentleman that worked in the same room he worked in, C.J., would speak to me a lot more than Tony would. Of course I saw him daily, but I didn't care to see him outside of the school. I taught the use of the machines that he repaired. He was polite, tall and handsome but I didn't even think of him in regards to all of that.

Most of the time I was off duty, I would either go to the clubs with the few friends I had made, or go back to my room to ready myself for the next day, ironing my uniform or watching television. I wasn't big on writing letters, but I missed my darling children, with every bone in my body. It seemed that every minute I was without them I grew more disappointed in my fight to get back with them. Once I got over the hangover I would become the instructor that the army paid me to be. I would swear I would never drink again. Once I got off duty I would head straight to the liquor store. I still had my battle dress uniforms (BDU) on. When I got out of the liquor store, I was trying to get the bottle open, and get out of those BDUs, while I drove, not caring which came first. Okay, maybe opening the bottle was first. Of course I would get drunk, and about ten o'clock I'd be passed out, and on, and on… One day I was introduced to my friend's friend, Carman. Carman lived in an off post trailer. We would get high off marijuana and liquor in that trailer all the time after work.

Carmen and I had a lot in common so we became best friends. We got along so well that we decided to get an apartment together. The agreement was that we would split everything she would give me her half, and I would pay the bills. She had a job at one of those stop and shops. Two months after we moved in she said they fired her. She seemed as if she was so depressed, and worried about not upsetting me about her portion that I assured her, "Girl you will find a job, I can cover the bills while you looked. It won't take you long before you get another job. We'll be okay for a while."

Instead of a job, she brought home a boyfriend who came by every day, drank our beer, and ate the food in our refrigerator. I didn't care about them being together, but he was an E5/SGT like I was, but I was paying all the bills, and Carman had stopped looking for a job all together. I told Carman that I was moving out, and they could keep the apartment. I went through the process of getting a one bedroom apartment. I soon moved out, and into my own place. I guess she didn't believe me when I told her I was moving. I enjoy a drama free environment so when she came banging on my door, and swearing at me; I decided not to answer the door.

Carman was known for carrying a switchblade, and I liked my face the way it was. When she finally stopped banging on my door, I knew it wasn't over. I went to the window, and true to Carman's reputation, I witnessed her using the switchblade on my car tires. I just laughed with my friend who was with me that night. David asked me, "Why are you laughing at her cutting your tires?" I answered, "I knew she was packing, and I have insurance on the car. I would much rather she cut my tires, than my face, and also, I'm insured."

Of course, I looked at my car the next day, and I was not happy with what I saw. She had cut all four of my tires. I called my insurance company but the deal was I had to take out a warrant on her before they would fix the tires. I thought this was fair enough so this is what I did. Police must have picked her up, because that following night they picked me up on the warrant; solicitation of sexual sodomy, I had to look that one up. She was trying to hurt my reputation in the military. I couldn't believe it. I was shocked to believe I was actually in jail. When I realized I was in jail. I decided it was because I tried to trust someone, and because of that trust someone got close enough to me where they thought they could manipulate me.

I tried to have a friend, and help someone when they were down. Because of this I was actually in jail. I called a friend, Larry to get me out. He didn't ask me any questions which was fine with me. It was embarrassing to let someone know what was going on in my life. Especially with the charges made against me. She didn't appear to any of the court appearances so they threw out the charges. I never got in a situation like that again. No more sharing of apartments for me. Larry dropped me off at home and I thanked him. I don't think he could ever understand how grateful I truly felt that night.

Going to the Chapel; 1983

"Wah Mee massacre:¹¹⁶" thirteen people were killed in an attempted robbery in Seattle, Washington, U.S. *"Environmental Protection Agency¹¹⁷"* announced its intention to buy out, and evacuate the *"dioxin-contaminated¹¹⁸"* community of *"Times Beach, Missouri,¹¹⁹"* a special commission of the *"Congress of the U.S.¹²⁰"* released a report critical of the practice of *"Japanese internment¹²¹"* during *World War II. "Strategic Defense Initiative:¹²²"* U.S. President Ronald Reagan, makes his initial proposal to develop technology to intercept enemy missiles. The media dub this plan Star Wars *"Sally Ride¹²³"* becomes the first American woman in space, on the Space Shuttle Challenger, *"America West Airlines*124" begins operations out of Phoenix, Arizona, and Las Vegas, Nevada. The *"United Kingdom general election, 1983:*125" Conservative Margaret Thatcher, Prime Minister of the United Kingdom since 1979, wins in a landslide victory over Michael Foot (forty-two per cent of the popular vote), the most decisive election victory since 1945.

U.S. President Ronald Reagan announced that the *"Global Positioning System (GPS)¹²⁶"* would be made available for civilian use, the rock group *"Kiss¹²⁷"* officially appeared in public without makeup for the first time on MTV. Simultaneous *"suicide truck-bombings¹²⁸"* destroyed both the French, and the United States Marine Corps barracks in Beirut, killing two hundred and forty-one U.S. servicemen, fifty eight French paratroopers, and six Lebanese civilians, at the White House Rose Garden, U.S. President Ronald Reagan signs a bill creating a federal holiday on the third Monday of every January to honor American civil rights leader *"Martin Luther King Jr.,¹²⁹"* the *"Reverend Jesse Jackson,¹³⁰"* announced his candidacy for the 1984 Democratic Party Presidential Nomination, the anticancer drug *"etoposide[131]"* was approved by the FDA, leading to a curative treatment regime in the field of combination chemotherapy of *"testicular carcinoma.[132]"* *"Brinks Mat[133]* robbery:" In London, six thousand, and eight hundred gold bars worth nearly UK£26 million are taken from the Brinks Mat" vault at Heathrow Airport. Only a fraction of the gold is ever recovered, and only two men are convicted of the crime.

One day, while at home in my newly acquired apartment, I was reading what people classified as a dirty book. There was a knock on my door, and when I answered it Larry, the old friend that had gotten me out of jail, was smiling back at me. He had Tony with him. He said they were just wondering what I was doing tonight so they came by to see me. Well. I wasn't doing anything worth mentioning, so I wasn't about to let them go. Loneliness does a lot of different things to a person.

I was so happy to see someone that night. We sat around and talked, drank and had a great time. Larry, who was married to a wonderful woman, made his excuses to leave but Tony stayed. It seems that after that night, Tony and I never left each other's side. Even when we were at work, I would stop by his work area, and he would give me his lunch order. He was a civilian so his lunch hours were only a half an hour long, whereas I was an NCO, so I could go to the nearby restaurants to pickup our orders so we could eat together. After work, I would wait on him to leave his work station. It really struck me as funny that the civilians had to watch the clock to strike three before they could leave. We would go to my apartment where we would not leave until it was time to go to work again. In other words, we became a couple.

I soon realized that I loved him so much; I would do almost anything for him. I say almost anything because there was one thing I couldn't do; that was forget my children. I was with him for about two months when I knew it had to be brought up. I loved him, and I knew he loved me… he had to love my children also. He and I could pool both of our money together, and between the two of us, we would be able to bring them to Georgia, have a pretty good lifestyle, and raise them as a family.

I didn't want to bring them here just to send them back again. I remember, we were still in bed, after making love. I turned to him, and asked him, "Tony, do you think you would have a problem with my bringing the children down to live with us." He turned to me, and said, "Sissy, I love you. If you want to bring the children down to add to our world together, there is nothing wrong with that. I love you, so I know I will love them. The sooner the better because if this is what will make, and keep you happy, so be it. I'm not going anywhere." I knew then that I had the greatest man in the world. It was around this time that we decided to make it official, by getting married. I did want the children to meet him prior to our getting married, but it just didn't seem important, since I knew they would love him as much as I did. We both took the day off; it was Friday, May 13, 1983. He wanted to marry me as much as I wanted to be his wife. It was a private ceremony, just the two of us.

We went downtown, and had a judge marry us. Neither of us could be happier that day. Once the marriage was in place, our next mission was to get a larger apartment so the children would have separate bedrooms. Thomas was twelve years old, and Dee was nine years old. It wasn't long after this that my dream of having my family together again was finally in place. I was a very happy woman. This only made me realize further, how wonderful this man I married was. Tony and I decided to have another baby, or should I say "I decided." I have to admit he had children from other women that he failed to support or visit, but I felt he would be different to our child. I wanted to have Tony's baby.

He always treated my other children so fatherly that I wanted to have a child which was created by both his and my blood. Since Deidra was the baby for ten years I felt that maybe it would be difficult for her to accept the change. I asked her, "How would you feel if you had another brother or sister?" She immediately jumped up and said she approved. I wanted to have his child but I had been warned, by my doctors after having Deidra, not to get pregnant again. My blood pressure rose so high when I had Deidra, the doctors didn't think I would live through another pregnancy. But I wanted this man's child so much. I pleaded, and begged him until he finally agreed.

One Drink After Another; 1984

It was 1984, the *"Cosby Show,[134]"* debuted on NBC, *"Michael Jackson's[135]"* hair caught fire during the filming of a Pepsi commercial, *"Marvin Gaye[136]"* died after being shot by his father the Reverend Marvin Gay Sr, *"Michael Jordan[137]"* joined the NBA signing with the Chicago Bulls, *"Purple Rain[138]"* the album, and the movie made *"Prince[139]"* a superstar, Miss America, *"Vanessa Williams[140]"* (NY) / *"Suzette Charles[141]"* (NJ), was crowned. There were two that year since there was a scandal concerning Vanessa Williams, *"Apple[142]"* introduced the user-friendly *"Macintosh[143]"* personal computer, the "acquired immune deficiency syndrome144" (AIDS) virus, was identified, the government ordered *"air bags[145]"* or *"seat belts[146]"* are required in cars by 1989, and when Melissa was born, I felt my life was complete. She came within the time frame the doctors said she would, and it wasn't as fearful as the doctors had indicated. Since I was afraid to let anyone take care of my six week old baby, I was contemplating whether to get out of the military.

Once my six weeks convalescence was over I had to report in to let my command know what my decision was. It was pretty much taken out of my hands when I reported back to work. I was told I had a six month duty assignment as the Noncommissioned Officer in Charge (NCOIC) of the child care center, on the military post. I must have been good to my chain of command. Someone within my command had to make this decision in my favor. I was so happy to know they were looking over me like this. My assignment was the solution to my dilemma. Now my baby would be in the next room. The women that took care of her would now work for me.

When we were in Georgia, we enjoyed going out to the clubs to play pool, while we drank. Tony started acting out after he drank too much. I never gave him any reason to merit his accusations but it didn't stop him from believing his fears. He was constantly accusing me of seeing other men behind his back, which I wasn't. I had stopped going out with him because when we did go out, he would be aware of some man looking at me.

Then instead of telling the person to stop looking at me, which I thought would have been ridiculous anyway, his reaction was to start an argument with me, for someone looking at me. As long as I didn't go out with him it seemed to quiet his jealousy. The problem with this was I now drank while I was at home around the children. Thus, making my drinking time to be more often since I didn't wait until I went out. Between my going to work, and drinking at home, it seemed time flew by. I'm not really sure what my children were doing during this time.

It was 1986 when we again went to Germany. The time went by so rapidly. It was probably healthier for the family to be in another country, since we were drinking so much that the children were raising themselves about now. This time I was allowed to take my family. Tony picked up a job with the civilian contractors in Germany. With both of us working, our life was the perfect family. Melissa was a very happy child, and when she smiled the whole room would glow. I had not prepared myself for what was going to take place during the rest of my life. As I got older, my dreams started shifting away from what I wanted for me, to what I wanted for them. After the children went to school, I was no longer Sissy.

I was Deidra's mom; Melissa's mom. I joined churches, and attended schools according to the programs they had set up for my children, and went to the school functions, according to what my children were involved in. I think you get the ideal; especially if you're a mom. During this tour to Germany my two year old daughter got a hold of my X1-12. I wasn't sure how many pills she had taken, if any, but I knew I had to get her to the doctor as soon as possible. When we took her to the German medical hospital, I was candid about what she took. This was my daughter so no matter what happened to me, they had to save her. The hospital told us that because of the way Melissa was acting, they felt she hadn't taken many of the pills.

They didn't feel it necessary to pump her stomach. They did tell us to keep an eye on her overnight, and return if we felt Melissa was getting worse. After this incident I poured out the rest of the little red pills that looked like M&Ms. Although, I knew this didn't mark the end of my use with hashish, booze or marijuana. I guess I was a selective addict. When my family was scheduled to return to the United States, we really weren't ready to go. We enjoyed Germany, so it just wasn't the time for us to go. We had spent three years in Germany, and it was time to go. But as the orders were cut, we had no choice. My children said their goodbyes to their friends, and my husband and I made the plans necessary to depart for our next duty assignment. With everything around us going on, we did (begrudgingly), get on the plane.

Enough, of the Madness; 1989

George H. W. Bush succeeded Ronald Reagan as the *"forty-first President of the United States of America,[147]"* Ron Brown was elected chairman of the *"Democratic National Committee,[148]"* he became the first African American to lead a major U.S. political party, in the Soviet war in Afghanistan: The *"Soviet Union[149]"* announced all of its troops had left Afghanistan. The *"Pan Am Flight 103[150]"* investigators announced the cause of the crash was a bomb hidden inside a radio-cassette player. In regard to gun control; U.S. President George H. W. Bush *"banned assault weapons[151]"* from being imported into the United States, in *"Alaska's Prince William Sound[152]"* the *"Exxon Valdez oil spilled[153]"* two hundred and forty thousand barrels (eleven million gallons) of oil after running aground, the U.S. government seized the Irving, CA Lincoln Savings and Loan Association; involving Charles Keating (for whom the *"Keating Five[154]"* were named – John McCain among them) eventually Keating went to jail, as part of the massive 1980s Savings and Loan Crisis which cost US taxpayers nearly two hundred billion dollars in bailouts, and many people their life savings.

The *"Ayatollah Khomeini died in Iran;[155]"* during the funeral, his corpse fell out of the casket into the mob of mourners, a federal grand jury indicted Cornell University student Robert Tappan Morris, Jr. for releasing a computer virus, making him the first person to be prosecuted under the *"1986 Computer Fraud and Abuse Act,[156]"* *"Space Shuttle Columbia[157]"* took off on a "secret five-day military mission," U.S. President George H. W. Bush held up a bag of cocaine purchased across the street at "Lafayette Park,158" in his first televised speech to the nation, *"F. W. de Klerk[159]"* was sworn in as State President of South Africa. In the Cold War; *"Günter Schabowski[160]"* accidentally stated in a live broadcast press conference that new rules for traveling from *"East Germany to West Germany[161]"* will be put in effect immediately, East Germany opened checkpoints in the Berlin Wall, allowing its citizens to travel freely to and from West Germany for the first time in decades, Germans to began tearing the wall down, South African President F.W. de Klerk announced the scrapping of the *"Separate Amenities Act.[162]"*

In a meeting off the coast of Malta, U.S. President George H. W. Bush and Soviet leader Mikhail Gorbachev released statements indicating that the Cold War between their nations may be coming to an end, *"Operation Just Cause[163]"* was launched in an attempt to overthrow *"Panamanian dictator Manuel Noriega[164],"* and I gave up alcohol and drugs.

We were greeted by friends at the airport in Georgia. Once we were settled in their home for a visit, we started talking about the events that took place while we were away. It was during this time that I first was told about the drug commonly known as Crack. Our close friend, George was now stationed in Korea. Larry and Clara told us that before he left, he, and his wife had been occasionally using crack. Now that George was in Korea, his wife, Lois was using the drug hard. She had been selling, and pawning almost everything in the house, and she was looking bad.

Lois was the type of woman that kept her appearance up. Some would even say she was high maintenance. This was no longer the case. Even the two children she had was showing the signs that mom was no longer taking the time to care for them in the manner which Lois usually was known for. The younger daughter was wearing glasses which were held together with a military rubber band (called a boot blouse; it keeps your pants tied high on your boots). Wouldn't be so bad if the optometrist wasn't right on the post where we lived. Our military benefits would financially cover the repair. She would just have to make some time to take the child to the optometrist.

Larry and Clara were speaking of the problem as if it was something neither of us could do anything about. My husband and I looked at each other as though we were responsible, at least as friends, to do something to help. I asked Larry and Clara if they had the phone number to George in Korea. Once we had the number, we called him, and told him he had better get back to Georgia, to help his family. We explained what the situation was, as we understood it. George thanked us, and within days he was shipped back to Georgia on a hardship tour. I wasn't there so I can't say how he accomplished it but soon his family was back, in the ways that counted. Lois again looked like the stunning black woman she had always been.

Their young daughter was wearing new glasses, and they hadn't pawned the family dog, which she had planned to do next. Lois had already groomed the dog to pawn it next. I'm sure there were really important things which had changed for the better, but this is the only thing that I was privy to see. I wished this was the end of my relationship with crack, but unfortunately I was destined to see more of it in my near future. Once we were assigned to post quarters in Georgia we had a pretty good life. I had decided that I needed to quit drinking after an incident I still don't remember.

The blackouts were coming more frequently, and I really didn't like the hangovers. One day my eldest daughter (Deidra); fifteen years old at the time, was sitting in a chair doing her homework. I could see scars on the lower part of her neck. I asked her to remove her blouse where I could see her torso. She did this, revealing more scratches. I asked her where and when she got them. She asked, "Mamma, you really don't remember the fight we got into last night?"

I definitely didn't remember, nor did I want to believe her. But she had no reason to lie, so of course I believed it. I swore to her that day, I would never drink again. I meant it too. I enrolled myself into a drug and alcohol treatment facility. It was an in-house treatment facility, and they didn't have a bed for me until June. I notified my chain of command of my decision, and they agreed it was a good idea. I guess they noticed my alcoholic behavior but just weren't saying anything. I waited for the call saying my bed was ready. I official stopped drinking on May 1, 1989. I had been in the field for two weeks, and I was bone tired when I heard a scream coming from the direction of downstairs. I had also just fallen into a deep sleep; I had been ill earlier so I was having trouble sleeping. The noise was coming from my son, Thomas, who by now had reached the door to my bedroom. He screamed, "Tony and one of his friends are in the kitchen killing each other."

I jumped out of my warm bed to rush into the kitchen from which the killing was taking place. I was prepared for just about anything except what I behold. My husband was sitting on one side of the kitchen table, his friend the other; much like arm wrestling. The difference was instead of arm wrestling, they were taking turns hitting each other in the face with their fists. Both of them were sloppy drunk. Blood was flying everywhere. These two fools were so proud of themselves, for being able to withstand the other's blows, and they were laughing after each blow. I felt they were acting like two immature fools that needed to back away from the bottle of booze, and get some sleep. I solved the problem by appealing to their fear of the military police upon them both. "If you two don't break up this ridiculous game, and go to sleep I will call the military police, and have you both hauled off. Tony put your friend in the guest room. I don't want him to drive so tell him I have his keys when he wakes up." As my husband wasn't moving fast enough to go to our bed, so I screamed, "I most definitely will call the military police if you don't move now."

It was around this time that I started regretting my decision to stay with Tony. Although I had given up getting high, smoking and drinking, obviously my husband had not. These various incidents lead up to our demise and made it apparent that we could not stay together. The final straw was pulled when his best friend, Anthony, came to our house. He was departing from his visit with Tony, and I just happened to be outside when he came out to get in his car, so I said goodbye with a hug. He got into his car, and drove away. Upon his leaving Tony came over to me, said, "I saw you flirting with Anthony." The next thing I knew he punched me in my eye. I had just been enrolled in a leadership class which attendance was mandatory.

Now I had to go to school with a black-eye. Of course I was upset about the other implication but, "A black-eye!" and for something I didn't do. I loved this man with all my heart, but his jealousy was getting out of hand. I didn't do anything to justify his actions. I told him, "Tony, this is ridiculous. I can't continue in this relationship without trust." He said, "I know. I don't know why I feel so much jealousy." I said, "Maybe if you stopped drinking so much you could control it." I continued, "Tony, I love you, but I can't do this." We ended the relationship amicably, and remained friends.

Can't We Just Get Along; 1991

It was 1991, the *"Gulf War[165]"* in Iraq invaded Kuwait, which eventually lead to the Gulf War, also called Desert Storm/Desert Shield. U.S., President George H. W. Bush, delivered a nationally televised speech in which he threatened the use of force to remove Iraqi soldiers from Kuwait, the U.N. Security Council passed the *"U.N. Security Council Resolution 678,[166]"* authorizing military intervention in Iraq if the nation did not withdraw its forces from Kuwait, and free all foreign hostages by the following Tuesday. January 15, 1991, Saddam Hussein released the *"Western hostages,[167]"* "U.S. President George H. W. Bush," and the *"Soviet Union, Leader Mikhail Gorbachev[168]"* signed a treaty to end chemical weapon productions, and began destroying their respective stocks.

East Germany and West Germany reunified into a single Germany, agreeing to merge currency, and economies, the S.U. Leader Mikhail Gorbachev, were awarded the *"Nobel Peace Prize,[169]"* for his efforts to lessen the Cold War tensions, and reforming his nation. *"Nelson Mandela[170]"* was released from Victor Verster Prison, near Cape Town, South Africa, after twenty seven years behind bars, American mob boss, *"John Gotti,[171]"* was arrested, the *"World Health Organization[172]"* removed homosexuality from its list of diseases, *"Homosexual acts,[173]"* between consenting adults are decriminalized in Queensland.

"U.S. President George H. W. Bush[174]" signed the *"Americans with Disabilities Act,[175]"* designed to protect disabled Americans from discrimination, U.S. President George H. W. Bush, posthumously awarded Jesse Owens the *"Congressional Gold Medal[176]," "Douglas*

Wilder[177]" became the first elected African American governor as he took office in Richmond, Virginia, James Buster Douglas knocked out Mike Tyson, to win the *"World Heavyweight Boxing[178]"* crown. Evander Holyfield defeated James Buster Douglas, for the *"Heavyweight Boxing[179]"* crown, Microsoft released *"Windows 3.0,[180]"* U.S. President Bush broke his 1988 *"no new taxes[181]"* campaign pledge by accepting tax revenue increases as a necessity to reduce the budget deficit. This greatly decreased his popularity in subsequent years. *"Tim Berners-Lee[182]"* published a more formal proposal for the World Wide Web (www).

Tony had never shown any telling behavior in regards to crack until I received orders to return to Germany. Tony and I were having a difficult rift in our marriage. My solution was to stop using everything, such as alcohol, cigarettes, etc. I didn't even know about the drug known as "Crack." He continued using everything and I soon discovered much more. This year was a very turbulent year for the country as well as for me. When I did decide to get the divorce, I had no trouble from him. He was such a proud man; he didn't want to stay where he wasn't wanted, but his credit was bad so he couldn't get an apartment. I went, and got one for him, turned on the phone, and electricity in my name. When I returned home, I gave him the keys with the agreement that he would take my name off everything after the first six months. He took the keys, and left. The separation wasn't good for me, so I would stop by his apartment under the gaze of checking on him, and taking him a cooked meal.

I came down on orders, and was sent to Germany again. This tour was well received since I was able to take my children with me. They were able to go to a school in Germany on Post in the vicinity of where we lived. When I arrived to my duty assignment, I was placed in charge of the section, which was accepted by all the subordinate personal, but not the assigned Noncommissioned Officer (NCO)'s...

The unit I worked with was several miles from my headquarters, so if we needed to see the commander or the first sergeant we had to drive there. I was the person in charge of our area, since I was the Senior Noncommissioned Officer in Charge (SNCOIC). This was arranged by the joint decision of the Company Commander and me, after I witnessed the actions of the other two NCOs. They were staff sergeants like me but they demonstrated poor leadership characteristics. Mainly they weren't covering each other's ass like I felt good NCOs should do.

The present NCOIC was well pass his weight limit, and the other was being charged with an Article 15 (military disciplinary action), for leaving her place of duty without proper authorization. They were poor examples for the subordinate personnel, as well as the other NCOs assigned. I knew I could be a better leader. It wouldn't take much for improvement since their actions were so inexcusable. I knew one thing was sure; I didn't want either of them covering my rear extremity. I always agreed with the motto, "If you're not a part of the solution, then you're a part of the problem."

I went to Kaiserslautern, and explained all this to the commander, who in turn agreed with me. The commander placed me in charge of the community's military post, which was a lot of responsibility. Being in charge of this many soldiers made it vital to be sober. I was on-call all of the time. I don't think I would have made it, if I was still drinking like I had been prior to this duty assignment. It was unfortunate for me to be in charge of an NCO, that was the same rank as I, but I did out-rank her by time in grade. Although she was my junior in time in grade, by at least nine months, she was vindictive in nature. She was also immature in my eyes, which is why I did not trust her, and I had write her up for several infractions, in the attempt to counsel her.

When I got a request from the First Sergeant to come to the Kaiserslautern Headquarters, it was a little surprising. Kaiserslautern was a good hour's drive. Also, usually the only way people got summoned from Zweibruecken, to the battalion in Kaiserslautern, is when I requested it. When I got there, the first sergeant told me this was an official visit which he was going to keep between me, and him. One of my people (like I didn't know who it was), had made copies of some personal correspondences (very explicit love letters to my boyfriend, stationed in Korea).

I had typed it on my official computer which we were not suppose to do. My subordinate was the NCO I had counseled earlier. She snooped into my computer, found the letters, and sent them to the Commander. My first sergeant was unofficially giving me a verbal counseling, to be followed by a written one if this happened again. We both knew the source, but neither that nor the reason why she did it mattered. She was in the right this time; I had no right to use an official computer for personal business. I only got away with this infringement because of my hard work, and my reputation. Even when I didn't retaliate against her, her back stabbing ways did not stop there. Some people just don't know when to leave well enough alone.

Deidra and Melissa enjoyed the adventure of new schools, meeting other people, and getting adjusted to the new environment. Thomas on the other hand, didn't find this adventure exciting enough. He had an adventure of his own to partake into. It started one day, after I came back home, after three weeks in a military training exercise in the field. He asked if he could use the car, when I was in bed, tired, and sleepy. It didn't occur to me to say no. Thomas was eight teen years old, and he had his international driver's license.

I was sound asleep when I heard the phone ringing through my sleep. I answered it to discover that my car had been impounded in Kaiserslautern Germany. The German police had taken my son, and four other young men into the custody of the Kaiserslautern, German police. I woke up real fast after this phone call. It was about three o'clock in the morning so I knew there wasn't much I could do, but I was in shock that all of this was happening. How could Thomas be in jail, much less in a German jail? It then occurred to me, "Where were my daughters?" I got up, and went to their room. I discovered them in their beds, sound asleep. This was a relief. I still worried about Thomas, and why was my car impounded. It took at least two days to piece out the chain of events that lead to the answers for these questions.

It seemed that Thomas, being the eldest of the boys involved, had gotten hold of a case of beer... with my keys in hand he, and the other three young men had decided to drive down to the town named Kaiserslautern; by the time they arrived they were all drunk. They seem to have raised havoc in this town, and were arrested; their parents were notified, they all were given a court date, and returned to their parents that next day. On the other hand, although the age for adulthood in Germany was twenty one, Thomas was being held as an adult.

Thomas was the eldest of the boys; he supplied the booze, and was in possession of the vehicle used that night. He was to be held in a German jail located in Mannheim, for six months prior to the court date. This was an additional burden on me. I would go every

Wednesday to visit him, and give him updates on his case. Most of the other people, whether they were prisoners or not, spoke little if any English. Wednesday was the only day they had a German translator available. Without a translator the prison authorities would not let him have visitors. It seemed they didn't want Thomas talking to anyone; not even his mother, unless they could understand what we were saying.

The exception to this, of course, was his lawyer. We were provided an American lawyer and a translator. It seemed that he was to be given time served and handed back to the hands of the US Government. Although it didn't feel like my unit blamed me for my son's behavior; I was given two weeks to return him back to America. Thomas had finally been released from jail. The German judge had determined that although they felt Thomas was responsible for the incident. They didn't have enough evidence to find him guilty so they released him to me with time served.

The Battalion Commander explained to me why Thomas could not stay in Germany. This was by order of the Brigade Commander. The government had deemed him an embarrassment to the United States of America, so evidence or not, he was going back to America. It was a godsend that I knew some old friends that he could stay with while I completed my tour in Germany. After the incident with Thomas, time seemed as if it just flew by. Deidre and Melissa were growing so fast. Melissa had gone from elementary school to junior high for Melissa and high school to College for Deidre. Deidre would spend many hours in her room and when she did come out it was to ask me if I would do something she had already committed me for or to ask if she could leave.

You Need Me-I Need You; 1993

Melissa was still my little girl, always running to me with her problems, whether big or small, but mostly to hug me or let me know in other ways how much she cared. She was so sensitive when it came to anything in need, animals or people. When we were reassigned from one military post, Zweibruecken, Germany to another one, Heidelberg, Germany, Deidre went off to college in Augsburg Germany. That left Melissa and me to carry on, so to speak. It was around this time that Tony called. I guess it didn't seem like he was divorced until he saw he couldn't get to Germany without his passport. I, despondently, listened as he relayed his situation in Georgia. "Sissy, I seem to have gotten myself into a bit of trouble. I've started using crack. I've lost my car, I owe money on this apartment, and I even have a felony charge hanging over my head for driving under the influence again. I still have a job, but that seems to be just barely. Please help me to get out of this mess. I had no idea how much I needed you."

He basically said he needed my help to get out of the states. He wanted to get away from the drugs that were so easily accessible in the states. "Even if you just have some ideas as to how I can fix any of this mess; I respect your opinion." As I listened to him rattle off his recent discretions I thought how ridiculous and irresponsible it would be for me to jump back into his world of insanity. He was bad news, and with each word he spoke he proved to me how right I was.

I remembered each time he did something wrong, in my opinion, and I called him on it, he would always turn it around to say something like, "Well you did it too." This would irritate me to no end, seeing as how I had never done the deed we were talking about. It worked for him; I didn't want to be confrontational to him anymore after these comments, so I would walk away or hang up the phone. I was shocked because he would never admit that he was wrong or responsible for anything in the past. This was his nature.

It was always someone else's fault, or he just didn't do it. I was surprised to hear him talk this way. I was thinking, "He must really need me, and this must mean he learned his listen as he hit bottom, or he knew this was long distance so he didn't want to defeat his cause by starting an argument with me." I thought about the good days when our love was strong. I thought about the fact that he was Melissa's father, and I thought about what he would do if the table was turned around. He was my best friend.

I told him that I was scheduled to depart Germany so I was granted thirty days leave time. I would come to Georgia at that time, and we could see what we wanted to do then. We would also discuss other ways to solve his main problems, which was crack. With the phone call from Tony hanging over my head, I had many things to think about. Although I was not sure whether I would bring him overseas, I did get the First Sergeant to approve the updating of his passport, and providing a set of orders in Tony's name.

I also had my tour to Germany changed to an accompanied tour. My tour changed from a two year to a three year tour but it was worth it as long as I had my family with me. This meant I could now have my family with me, I know I had a control issue but this brought me peace of mind. The change allowed me to receive a passport, and the orders I would need for Tony's travel on an airplane to get back to Germany with me. It was about time for us to take a leave from the military life anyway. Melissa and I were happy to be going home on leave. I really didn't know what I was going to do or say to Tony, but he was forever on my mind. We were divorced, and for that matter, it was for good reason. I still remember the black eye. But if anyone asked me, yes I still loved him. It was like looking at a cute dog and wanting to pet it.

Unfortunately the dog is not willing to have you pet it, and as you reach your hand out, it bites you. Only a fool would want to pet it again. I'm not going to lie; call me a fool because as soon as I came close to Tony, the old feelings returned, and I felt the heat of our love racing through my body. I know a lot of it was lust, but I really did love this man, and I wanted to take him in my arms and protect him. He told me everything about how he got involved with crack, and how he thought he could handle it. I asked him, "People told you the stories about it only taking one time to get hooked.

Everyone else you know, who tried it, felt they could handle it prior to getting hooked also. What made you think you wouldn't get hooked? Was the thought of the high being good really worth the consequences of taking this chance?" I continued my tirade with, "I have yet to understand the "not me" syndrome. People who take that first hit somehow seem to think it can't happen to them. They have this attitude that although they hear of so many people getting hooked on crack, it can't happen to them. I understand that once you hit the first high, you continue to seek that high again, and again. Do you think I'm going to try it? Hell no.

People, like you that feel they are stronger than others or immune to something want to glimpse into what the other people felt. Then after you are hooked, you want to understand what made this drug so powerful." Tony knew there was no answer to my frustration so he went on with his explanation of how he was working with a district attorney that agrees to let him leave the country if he pays so much money. This was due to the driving under the influence charges pending over him. Although I hadn't said anything about letting him return to my life, we talked, and proceeded to get his life back into some type of order.

I'm not even sure what happened to put me back into the situation; I know I opened my heart to his desires, and soon I found myself back into his arms. I can't say I didn't know what I was getting myself into, because he told me how bad it had been for him. He told me he wanted to quit smoking crack, and return to the lifestyle we once lived. I fell deep into the fantasy of thinking that life could be restarted. Just as he felt he could be stronger than crack.

I started to believe that he could perform a redo. We decided that the first thing we needed to do was get remarried. We, Melissa, Tony, and I, drove to Milwaukee, Wisconsin, where my parents were located. This time we were going to do it right. The pastor of my father's church was going to preside over it, in front of my mother, father, two sisters, and a couple of my brothers. We were going to put it on with super glue, this time. Afterwards, we took the plane back to Germany where we began to revitalize our lives. We stayed in Heidelberg Germany, where life was a piece of cake.

Tony and I would take long walks in German countryside. He attained a job with the united state government civilian hire source, which was contracting work with the Germans. He enjoyed his work and talked of it often. I was so happy that I made the decision to reunite with Tony. Melissa was also happy to have her father back home. It was two years later in September when we received a phone call from the states. It was Monica that told me our Mom had a heart attack. Although we knew Dad had cancer, we felt he was okay with Mom taking care of him. Now that Mom was sick, we didn't have much choice than to return to the states.

Tony and I had been talking seriously about staying in Germany, since our lives were so happy. The decision to return to the states was a sad one. If we could have done it any other way, we would have. I requested a reassignment, due to an emergency so I could be there for my family. The military had sent us to Washington, DC, to work in the pentagon. The duty was fine, but Mom and Dad were in Milwaukee, Wisconsin. My mother had a heart attack, and my father had cancer along with the surgery to his spinal cord, and into his brain. I was told of the Parkinson disease by his doctors. Tony and I drove to, and from Milwaukee, as many times as we could.

Here We Go Again; 1994

Historical events from 1994 were, the shooting which triggered the celebrated feud between East, and West Coast rappers which led to the killings of "*Shakur*,[183]" and B.I.G, Tonya Harding won the national "*Figure Skating Championship*[184]" title, but was stripped of her title following an attack on her rival, Nancy Kerrigan, "*OJ Simpson*[185]" fled police in his white ford bronco, Lisa Marie Presley married "*Michael Jackson*,[186]" and I received from the probate court in Milwaukee, permission to be my father's executor for his estate.

Permission to be executor for my father's estate was necessary since my father was now in a coma, which I knew he was not coming out of. I knew this from the days when I acted as an in-home Nurse's Aide, holding the hand of dying patients. Their family members didn't want their family member to go alone. I was given permission to work when I was off duty from the military by the commander. My father had put some money aside, in his bank account, to be used in the event of his death. He did not have anyone else named on his bank account for authorization to get the money out. If he died prior to someone getting appointed as the executor, the money would go to his estate since even a power of attorney dies with the person approving it.

It was 1995 before I became executor to my father's financial estate; I had used the money to bury my father, and placed some money needed for mom's funeral in a trust so no one could spend it before she passed away. I knew my father wanted to ensure him and Mamma's funerals were taken care of without causing his children to pass the hat around, so to speak. He took care of his financial obligations in life and that is what he wanted in death. I had also taken out an insurance policy on my mother, to make up for any other bills that may have arisen.

Being named the executor of my father's estate allowed the banks to release the funds to me. I felt this was a great honor, my parents had placed in my hands, so I felt obligated to do what I believed my father would have wanted me to accomplish with his money. I divided the money in three ways; first there was the immediate need of having my father buried, which was used within one week after I got the executor appointment. I purchased an irreversible burial certificate for my mother, which I felt was my father's intention. I was sure he had this in mind when he saved this money. The rest of the money, which was five thousand dollars, I placed it in a checking account for my mother, in the bank daddy had used, but I insisted that my brother, Trey was named as an authorized user of the checking account, so he could assist her in getting things done around the house, and be there for her in her hours of need, prior to her passing away.

As I stated it wasn't long before my father died, and mom was diagnosed with cancer. I had a conversation with her, when I was home to bury my father. I was driving her to and from her doctors' appointment. I told her, "Mom you really have to take this cancer seriously." She replied, "Why? As far as I'm concerned, I'm ready to go. Momma, that is not funny." She returned, "Sissy, I am not trying to be funny. I really am ready to go." I said, "But momma, you have so much to live for. We're not ready to see you go." This was beginning to worry me. Is it because daddy is gone?" She looked at me, facing me as I drove, "Some of it, but I'm just tired.

It is not my intention to worry you. As far as you, and the others not being ready, that is your problem. You might as well get use to it." I pulled over to the curb, "Momma I can understand your grieving, since daddy just died; you cannot take the luxury to ignore this cancer. It is serious, and it is here. Please mom, think about it, and do the thing that is best for you." I don't know which one of us moving into the hug, but I enjoyed being so close to her. I really don't remember her ever hugging me before, and it was not going to happen again. Prior to leaving my mother's home, I was a witness to my brothers constantly drinking and getting high. There were other signs of addiction which were noticed. Such as their failure to be home when I was there. One of my brothers actually told me, "Those people are crack head; they are weak. I am so unlike them. Besides, as long as I can keep paying my telephone bill, smoking cocaine doesn't hinder me. I love getting high, and as long as I keep on keeping on, I will not stop." My home was no longer my home. Of course, I'm speaking of my family members and my old friends.

After dad's funeral, I returned to my duty assignment in Washington, DC, with duty in the Pentagon. I decided this was the time to get things ready for our final move since I would soon retire from the military. I took the long route back to the Pentagon; I took the route through Alabama. The preparations for buying a home in Alabama seemed to be effortless. I had hired a realtor to take me around. After I found the house, I hoped to get Mom to come to Alabama, to at least see what I had accomplished though out the years, with her help. I had been away from home for twenty years so of course I missed her. My children and my future had been changed for the better thanks to my parents, mostly momma.

I found a home for them which to me, was so much better than I could ever have found in Washington, Virginia or Milwaukee. I bought the mortgage prior to returning to the Pentagon. It simply amazes me how some people think the glass is half-full and yet others know it's half-empty. People buy homes and stocks because they want to own a piece of the rock. Owning something makes people feel secure in their existence. I just wanted to show my mom how much I had accomplished.

Crack Takes a Stand; 1996

I soon got orders to go to Korea. Since this was my first tour to Korea, I was told this was an unaccompanied tour. I would be there for only a year. The night prior to getting on the plane for my tour of duty in Korea, I thought I spent a special night with Tony. We had fallen asleep on the carpet in front of the television. As we got up very early in the morning, so we could catch the flight to Korea, something fell out of his pants pocket. I asked Tony, "Why do you have that in your pants pocket?"

He said, "It's nothing." I said with sarcasm in my voice, "I didn't ask you what it was. I know what it is. Why is it in your pocket?" He meekly said, "It belongs to Derrick. I told him I'd hold it for him." Derrick was his younger brother. I told Tony, "I know you think I'm a damn fool, but I know that crack pipe doesn't belong to Derrick. I have to catch a plane to Korea in less than three hours and I don't have time for this. We will work it out later." I turned my back to him signaling the end of the conversation; for now anyway. I was contemplative in regards to the solution I felt my family needed to go into. Deidra was enrolled in A&M University; money was not importance at this time, in regard to my baby girl's health and safety. Thomas had left to enroll into the services. Melissa would stay here with her father. After the morning I departed for Korea, I had the feeling I'd be back. I knew I needed to really fix things but I couldn't perform magic. I couldn't deal with this now. I had to report to my Korean headquarters.

I was a senior noncommissioned officer (SNCO) now. I now had my own quarters; a living area, and bedroom, along with a private bathroom. We had cable TV, a shower, microwave, and refrigerator. I must say it was nice; I just wished my children were with me. I worked hard for this unit that I had been assigned to. I no longer had the convenient distraction of my husband or children. I made a few friends; the ones I did make were similar in likes and dislikes. We went to the club on post; entertained each other in our rooms such as, playing chess or cooking for each other. Most of our days were spent on the roads between military installations in Korea.

I slowly started to enjoy my time in Korea; I had met a man that made me feel alive. He was my SNCO, his name was Ruben. Let it be said, we weren't supposed to fraternize. He had a woman back home which he intended to marry upon his arrival back home. We, at least I, didn't plan on having an affair. We went everywhere together. At first it was just his way of showing me around. We would walk to work, go to lunch at the mess hall, and later go out to the club to drink (I had mineral water), and socialize after work. One day, we went out to the club. Ruben had a friend from out of the area we protected for visiting the club. His name was Jackson. Ruben introduced me and his friend, Jackson, so we danced. I felt his friend was rude, and immature.

He was looking at my hair in the lights on the dance floor when he stated in a very loud voice, "Damn girl, how old are you? Look at all that grey hair!" Although I was forty six at the time, no one had ever called me on it. I was very good looking, if I say so myself, and my body was "*banging*" and I knew it. With all the walking, and physical training we were required to do, there wasn't time to worry about getting fat, or old. I was so disturbed by what he said that I left him on the dance floor. I returned to my table when Ruben asked me what was wrong. I told him nothing, but I said I was ready to leave. Ruben didn't bother to ask me why, he just got our coats and we left the club.

It was after we had left the club that Ruben inquired about whether I liked Jackson. I told him I did not. He was rude and he had the nerve to call me old." I also said, "Why are you trying to fix me up with people? I am quite content with the way things are." Ruben said, "I'm just trying to make you happy. I know you're married, but I thought you would appreciate some company." I asked him, "Sometimes I do want company, but why would you think you would have to look further than yourself?"

We do everything together. Are you tired of me hanging around?" He indicated, "No! Never! I love what we have. You're smart, and beautiful. I just thought you were tired of me hanging around, and I wanted to make you happy." He slipped right pass what I had said. Maybe he didn't understand what I said. Maybe he just didn't want to misread what I said, because he didn't want to jeopardize our relationship. "I know what you told me about your marriage. Do you think it's going to get better?"

I was having this conversation with Ruben, and it seemed inappropriate to discuss my fallen marriage with him when I had every intention of trying to work my magic on him. "Ruben, why haven't you tried to kiss me or anything?" He said, "Because you work for me and I didn't want it to affect our jobs." I said, "If I promise to keep it away from our jobs, would you like to kiss me? I don't want anyone else, Ruben." Ruben said, "I won't initiate it, but I couldn't fight it either." I took this to mean he wanted me too. We were in my quarters when I took his hand and placed it on my thigh. I leaned over, and kissed him. This was all I had to do because from the time I placed my lips on his I saw stars.

He leaned into the kiss. His hands were now all over my body. I felt my dress go up over my thighs but I didn't care. I just didn't want him to stop touching me. He leaned me back on the couch and suddenly he had his head between my legs. I hadn't felt this good in so long it felt like heaven. He rose over me and placed his manhood into me. It was so hot and big, I never wanted it to stop. But it did stop and both of us laid spent in our desires. This wasn't the only time I and Ruben made love. I wanted to keep him in my arms. I realized that I had lied to him. I couldn't keep it away from my job. I didn't fail to do my job, I'm too much of a professional to do that but I would think of him all day. I would walk to work thinking of him. I couldn't wait until he called, and we were together again.

As the Stomach Churns; 1996

One of the worst *"blizzards[187]"* in American history hit the eastern states, killing more than 150 people, Philadelphia, PA, received a record thirty point seven inches of snowfall. New York City's public schools were closed for the first time in eight-teen years, and the federal government in Washington, D.C. is closed for days. In the *"Whitewater scandal; U.S. First Lady Hillary Rodham Clinton[188]"* testified before a grand jury. Suspected *"Unabomber[189]"* Theodore Kaczynski was arrested. In Philadelphia, Pennsylvania, a panel of federal judges blocked a law against indecency on the internet. The panel says that the *"1996 Communications Decency Act[190]"* would infringe upon the free speech rights of adults.

"Iraq disarmament crisis:[191]" Iraqi forces refuse *"UNSCOM inspection team's[192]"* access to five sites designated for inspection. The teams entered the sites only after delays of up to seven-teen hours. UNSCOM supervised the destruction of Al-Hakam, *"Iraq's main production facility of biological warfare agents.[193]"* As Iraq continues to refuse inspectors access to a number of sites; the U.S. fails in its attempt to build support for military action against Iraq in the U.N. Security Council.

U.N. Inspector Scott Ritter attempts to conduct surprise inspections on the *"Republican Guard facility[194]"* at the airport, but is blocked by Iraqi officials. Iraqi forces launch an offensive into the *"northern No-Fly Zone,195"* and captured Arbil. The U.S. launches *"Operation Desert Strike[196]"* against Iraq in reaction to the attack on Arbil. UNSCOM inspectors *"uncovered buried prohibited missile parts.[197]"* Iraq refuses to allow UNSCOM teams to remove remnants of missile engines for analysis outside of the country, and I received a letter from Deidra; it outlined how their lives had taken a drastic change.

"Momma, daddy has started smoking crack again. He left us Thursday to go food shopping. It is now Sunday, and this house is still without food. We have been eating grits for most meals. Momma, we possess two cars, but he has torn up one, and stays gone with the other one, most of the time. I have a job in a grocery store, but I have to walk to work. When I get my paycheck I will be able to buy food, but that doesn't solve the problem of daddy. It seems like he's pawning things. I believe this since things around the house are disappearing." Deidra went on to write about how she felt, "Momma, it would be great if you could come home or at least send some money to me, please not to him. Don't bother calling, since the phone has been cut off." I took this news like a fist in the stomach. What was going on that she felt it necessary to write me a letter like this while I was in Korea completing my tour?

Of course I was going home. I told the First Sergeant what was happening back home, and he felt I had made the right decision. With the assistance of the Commander, I soon was on my way back to the states. Since the chain of command or myself didn't know what to expect, whether I was returning or not? I was granted a leave in conjunction with temporary duty which included training in a security class. This way I was allowed more time to get my family situated back in some kind of order. It was when I got the letter from Deidra that I opened my eyes to reality, I was aware that I either had to end it or make a decision to keep Tony. I had been putting it off for too long. It was as if the choice was taken out of my hands. I knew I couldn't leave Tony in the situation he was in.

This was when I told Ruben it had to end. I didn't want to, but I had to help Tony, after all he is my husband. Once again, it wasn't love that brought me back to Tony; it was the "crack." Somehow I knew Tony couldn't fight crack without my help. I had truly regretted having to release my love for Ruben. Not just the love making but everything we did together. I knew leaving Ruben would be difficult, but I had to bring my family back together. Unfortunately, I realized, that meant discontinuing my affair. As I watched Ruben walk away from me, I cried.

My tears were not because our affair or friendship was ending, but because I realized that the person I had grown to be was going to have to regress back to the woman I knew before. The woman I knew I really was. I had once again grown to be a woman in love with myself. The woman who; cared about her figure, as well as the inside transformation that was all of me. I had become someone that laughed a lot, and looked forward to seeing Ruben, not only at play but also at work. I thought about the fact that I would have to live my life like a housewife, and mother again, putting myself on the back burner again. I looked up at the Korean sky, and I cried.

I didn't want to give up Ruben. I didn't want to give up my nights at the club listening to jazz. I didn't want to lose this thin body I had acquired since I enjoyed myself, and the physical training that kept it this way, (physical therapy as we soldiers called it). I knew that if I returned to my pass existence I would lose all of this. But I knew I had to do the right thing. I had to save my family. My children meant everything to me. Not knowing what to expect, I took a cab from the airport to my home. As I walked into the house, it was dark, and quiet as a mouse. I placed my bags down on the floor, and with a smile on my face, and relief in my heart I yelled, "Isn't anyone going to help me with my bags?" Melissa was the first one down the stairs.

Melissa was screaming, and hugging me "Momma, you're home." She was crying with a smile on her face. Deidra was standing on the top of the stairs, staring at me; she also had a smile on her face. If I'm correct to believe, I could swear I heard a sign of relief come from her. She by now also had tears running down her eyes. As we lay on Melissa's bed they updated me on the events that brought me home. Melissa was the one that told me of the woman Tony had in our bed, one night. Melissa walked into the room to ask her father something, when the woman turned over, and her naked breast fell out of her cover.

She still had not awakened from a deep sleep. Tony did wake up, and I'm sure he felt embarrassed by getting caught in this predicament, and by no less than his daughter, Melissa. But instead of manning up, and talking to his daughter, who was by now scared, confused, and in pain, he shouted at Melissa to get the hell out of the room. She did so with tears in her eyes. She told me that he later tried to give her some lame excuse, but she wasn't buying it.

Unfortunately, for her, she wasn't aware of Tony's way of turning things around by saying, *"you did too;"* like it was your fault, rather than taking the blame for his actions. Deidra told of the times he went out to get groceries, and never returned throughout the weekend. Deidra was on summer vacation from college so she got a job a few blocks from the home. When there was no car at home, she would walk to work, leaving Melissa with the neighbors. Tony was nowhere to be found. Then there were also the times when Tony sent the car home with his drunken brother, who also had a woman with him that was wasted. Melissa was so embarrassed by her father's behavior; she didn't want to come home from her girlfriend's house.

Deidra told me of the time Tony was trying to take Melissa to Greenville, Alabama, with him. He had already been drinking, and he had liquor in the car. Deidra, very respectfully, told him he was not going to take Melissa with him in his condition. She was merely trying to protect her younger sister. In his mind she was being defiant, and he could only think of the times when he raised Deidra, as well as, Melissa. One thing led to another, when the next thing that happened was Deidra, and Tony wrestling on the ground. She even explained to me later that when he had his hands around her neck his hate toward her shining back at her from his eyes. Suddenly, for some unforeseen reason to her, he let her go, and she got up and pulled Melissa into the house, and in Melissa's room where they remained until he drove off.

I had heard enough, so I finally said, "Where is Tony?" Deidra said nothing, while Melissa said, as she pointed, he was in the master bedroom. I got up from the bed we were all sitting on. I turned, and said to them, with confidence, "Everything is going to be alright. I need to talk to Tony now but you guys need to know that we will all be fine, okay? You also need to get some sleep. We have a lot of work tomorrow." I said this 'okay' as a question, but they understood that I really wasn't waiting for an answer. I entered the room, and sat down next to a sleeping Tony. I tapped him, to wake him up.

He jumped up when he saw me, because one, he didn't know I was coming, and two, he was guilty as hell of what the girls told me. He was obviously coming down from a high. I knew the signs. "Tony, what's up, my love? I'm here to go to a security class that is being held at Fort Gordon, in Georgia. What have you been up too?" I said all of this to see what he had to say. I truly wanted to believe this whole incident was a figment of my daughters' imaginations. I prayed that he would open his mouth, and the magic words would fall out of his mouth to make this catastrophe go away. He would explain away the crack pipe that fell from his pants pocket the night I had to fly out of Birmingham, Alabama, to Seoul, Korea. The pipe, he said belonged to his only brother; not that I had any other choice but to get on the plane. No matter what I felt, I was a SNCO, and I knew the consequences of not getting on that plane. I had worked too hard for too many years to give it up now.

Unfortunately, nothing like the magic words I needed to hear was going to come from my husband that night. As a matter of fact, he was not going to say anything to clear up this situation. I asked him, "What have you been up to?" He said, "Nothing but trying to keep this house from falling apart. Why, what have you heard?" I decided to stop the exchange of niceties, and come straight to the point. I said, "Well I did hear something about you, and Deidra having a knock down drag out fight in front of the house. Melissa seems to remember some naked woman in our bed with you, and that was the high lights to the communication coming out of Alabama to Korea." He sat up in the bed to say, "Baby, if I had a knockdown, drag out fight in the front yard with Deidra, she would have more than a bruise on her. Do you see how much larger I am than her? I don't have an excuse for what Melissa saw. All I can tell you is she was just a friend. We got high and somehow ended up back here in bed. I swear I didn't touch her."

"You really believe that telling me nothing happened would get you out of hot water with me? I just traveled all the way from Korea due to some shit you are causing, and you really believe this is about some bitch in my bed? I am not naïve enough to think any of this is not caused by crack. You are on that shit again, and I'm not having it." Tony knew he had messed up, and it was time to return to the world of reality. I didn't want to leave Tony, but I truly believed that if he had fought me on this, I was ready to call it quits. I wasn't condoning his behavior in any way. I knew we had a lot of work ahead of us, and I was just trying to put my family back together once again.

We are Family; 1996

November 5, "*1996, U.S. Presidential Election: democratic incumbent[198]*" "*Bill Clinton defeated republican challenger Bob Dole[199]*" to win his second term. "*Mother Teresa[200]*" received honorary U.S. citizenship. "*Martin Bryant[201]*" was sentenced to thirty-five consecutive sentences of life imprisonment plus one thousand, and thirty-five years without parole for murdering thirty five people in a shooting spree in Tasmania earlier this year. U.S. President Bill Clinton signed the "*Electronic Freedom of Information Act Amendments.[202]*" "*HM the Queen[203]*" advised "an early divorce" to Lady Diana Spencer and Charles, Prince of Wales. The divorce was finalized on August 28, 1996.

"*Jon Benet Ramsey,[204]*" six, was murdered in the basement of her parents' home in Boulder, Colorado. "*Lyle and Erik Menendez[205]*" were sentenced to life in prison without the possibility of parole. "*Dolly the sheep,[206]*" the first mammal to be successfully cloned from an adult cell, was born. The "*1996 Summer Olympics[207]*" in Atlanta, Georgia, United States began. The "*Centennial Olympic Park bombing[208]*" at the 1996 Summer Olympics killed one and injured one hundred and eleven. U.S. President Bill Clinton and Vice President Al Gore are renominated at the "*Democratic National Convention[209]*" in Chicago. Bob Dole was nominated for President of the United States, and Jack Kemp for Vice President, at the "*Republican National Convention[210]*" in San Diego, California.

Thousands-large protest in "*Seoul, calling for reunification with North Korea,[211]*" was broken up by riot police. Former president of South Africa, F. W. de Klerk, made an official policy for crimes committed under Apartheid to the *"Truth and Reconciliation Commission[212]"* in Cape Town. *"Osama bin Laden,[213]"* wrote; "The declaration of Jihad on the Americans occupying the country of the two sacred places, a call for the removal of American military forces from Saudi Arabia." "The O. J. Simpson" civil trial began in Santa Monica, California.

When we woke up I told Tony with little emotion in my voice, "We are going to put this house up for rent with a realty company. Deidra is going back to school in Huntsville, Alabama. Melissa is going to come with me to Korea. I am going to enter you into a drug treatment center so you can get your shit together. Only, and I reiterate, only after you complete the program will you follow us back to Korea. Do you really have any questions?" He caught the tone in my voice, which was sarcastic, of course, because he said, "No, not really." We put Tony into a drug rehabilitation program.

I gave his passport, plane ticket, and fifty dollars to Clara with the instructions not to give it to him if he failed to commence or succeed in the program. I went to my training course, and Melissa stayed with me in a military hotel while I completed my classes. It was time for Deidra to go back to school so I gave her the 1995 Dodge, conversion van to go back and forth to her classes, and live in, if necessary. Deidra was to remain in the states to complete her degree. It didn't dawn on me that she would feel as if I were punishing her in some way. Years later, I discovered through her tears that she felt I had I chosen to save everyone by taking them with me, and left her to fend for herself. She felt that even Tony was chosen over her, and he caused the situation.

This tragic side of my actions was never even imagined until later in my life, when it was brought to my attention, by her. To tell the truth, I saw her point, but it was too late to change the past. What was done was done. I truly believed that if I had it to do over, I would still do the same things. She learned to fend for herself and grew into a wonderfully mature woman. I'm thinking that she was the one to benefit from the disaster. I just wished I had sat down to talk with her about what was going on. Made it clear to her how much I appreciated her candid ability to see the situation for what it was, and her strength to take care of the situation until she was able to get in touch with me, as she did.

Mom, Have it Your Way; 1997

In 1997 President Bill Clinton was inaugurated for his second term, Madeleine Albright became the *"first female Secretary of State,[214]"* after confirmation by the United States Senate, a jury sentenced Timothy McVeigh to death for his part in the *"1995 Oklahoma City bombing,[215]"* *and "Diana, Princess of Wales,216"* was taken to a hospital when she had a car accident shortly after midnight in Paris. She was pronounced dead at 4:00 AM, about six months into my one year tour to Korea, I had to change it to a two year tour.

A couple of months after I returned to Korea, my dream to get my mother to come to Alabama was drenched in sorrow when I was notified by my siblings that mom's cancer was all through her body. She refused to leave Milwaukee, even though my brothers were doing nothing for her. I heard stories of how my brothers were stealing her pain killers, and the money I had put in the bank was being depleted daily. I was so happy that I had decided to purchase her a burial trust. It was only a year later that my mother passed away.

She did this in her home, in her own bed, and under her own terms. Tony had just arrived to Korea so he was able to watch Melissa, in Korea while I went to Milwaukee. When I came to Milwaukee from Korea, my mother had not passed away so I felt blessed even though she was in a coma. My brother Trey had decided to put a new roof on the home with the remaining money. He wanted me to invest in this project. I told him that this would not be a good investment since Mom and Dad were departed, and the rest of the house was in bad shape.

After the funeral I went back to the house I use to call home. It took me returning from Korea to realize that six out of eight (one was dead) of my brothers were indulging in the substance called, "Crack Cocaine." With my mother, and father gone, it didn't feel like home. I really didn't know the boys, since we had nothing in common. I didn't smoke cigarettes, marijuana or drink liquor so that left me out of being where they were. I didn't know anything about the drug named, "Crack" except the episode our friends in Georgia had gone through, and the episode with Tony. I believe my brothers had more knowledge of it. Maybe more knowledge than they needed. No one came to see me while I was in the city. I felt as if they were hiding until I went back to Korea.

Once I had taken my inventory of my childhood residence, I spent the night with my Aunt Donna. The following morning, I pulled up to my mother's house. Just as I got out of my rental car the woman that handled my mother's life insurance policy got out of her car. I hugged her, and said, "Katharine, what are you doing here?" She said, "Your family called me. They have some questions." I smiled, "Well let's not keep them waiting." My five brothers and Paula gathered into the living room when we walked into the house. No one initiated the conversation. The room was silent, and it seemed like my presence had put a cramp in their plan.

Since no one seemed to want to take the initiative I spoke up, "Well, someone here had some questions in regard to the life insurance policy on Mamma. Katharine had to come down here because she was called. Could someone initiate this conversation so she can proceed with her work day? My brother, Charles, spoke up, "We just wanted to know how much it was taken out for, and how do we get the rest?" Katharine stated "Well, the policy was taken out by Sissy Smith, she is the beneficiary, and any further questions must be answered by Sissy Smith. That is all I can lawfully answer in regard to this policy. As I walked her to the door, I thanked her for everything she had done for me, and told her it was a pleasure meeting her, since prior to this I had only spoke to her on the telephone.

After she left, I turned to my family members, and said, "If you had any questions, I would have gladly told you what you wanted to know, if you had come to me, and asked. Since you have chosen to treat me like a stranger, by calling a stranger in to answer your questions, not to mention anyone made any attempt to assist me in paying the monthly premiums. I really don't see why you couldn't trust me to give you an honest answer. These are the reasons why I chose not to answer any further questions. I'm going to leave for Korea now." I did just that. I walked out of the house, and since my luggage had never left the trunk of the rental car, drove to the airport, dropped off the rental car and left. Now that both parents were gone, I knew I had no reason to come back to this place I use to call home. It was a short time after this occasion that I retired out of the Army. I'm not sure where or when it started, but my life started to take off in a direction I was not aware of how to control. I was soon shaken up by the people I loved. It seemed like the flood gates to hell had opened up.

"Crack's Destructive Force"

I didn't know the level of devastation crack had over, not only the people that indulged in it, but the people close to the addict. The people whose lives were linked to the addicts and the communities that became victims of this drug. From what I am told, crack cocaine is a freebase form of cocaine that is made using baking soda in a process to convert cocaine (powder cocaine) into freebase cocaine. The high usually lasts around 15 minutes, after which time dopamine levels in the brain plummet, leaving the user feeling depressed and low.

A typical response among users is to have another hit of the drug; however, the levels of dopamine in the brain takes a long time to replenish themselves, and each hit taken in rapid succession leads to increasingly less intense highs. The addicts are searching for that intense desire to recapture the initial high, which will never return, but that is what causes this addictive behavior for many users.

I discovered my son, Thomas, was smoking crack when Tony and I revisited my home city. Upon our return home, we looked at the truck outside, Tony had indicated, "It looks as if the truck has been moved." We thought nothing more of it. We went inside the house, and discovered all of our electronic equipment gone. All the televisions, VHS players, computers, and my baby girl, Melissa's electronic game was taken.

There was one thing that made it strange. Every room in the house was touched, except my room. The big screen television which had the VHS/DVD player was sitting in the exact spot they were sitting in when we left. It was only after we had reported the incidence, and the police came to our house that we were told what had happened. The officer told me I might want to sit down. I said to him, "Please tell me what you've found." He said, "We were contacted by the pawn shops that bought the computers, and televisions. The person that sold your property used your son's identification." I knew what he was saying; "You're saying that my son took all of our property and pawned it."

What to do with this information, I didn't know. I thanked the police officers, and Tony walked them to the door. We then sat down to deliberate what to do about Thomas. He wasn't home so it had to wait, but when he did come home we all had a pretty bad session. Thomas tried to deny it, "Momma, you know I wouldn't do that to you." He was so believable. When he was told the evidence, and how we received the evidence, he finally admitted to stealing the property.

"Momma, Dad, I did take it, but I couldn't help it. Please believe me. I need help." I told Thomas, "It would have been more believable if you would have made your plea before you took the stuff, rather than after." Tony and I decided to send him to a drug and alcohol program. This was the first of many that we were going to send him to in the immediate future. Tony and I went to the pawn shops that the police had directed us to, but the pawn shops would only sell us our property.

As we were standing outside trying to determine what our next move was going to be, Tony told me to look across the street. There across the street sat our Ford Mazda. It was sitting on some cement blocks. Thomas had also taken the wheels and rims off, and had sold them to the pawn shop. Thomas didn't have credit with the crack dealers to depend on, i.e., credit worthiness so he had resorted to stealing, and disappearing for a few days. Tony and Thomas had the same attitude when they first came down. They would be apologetic, and sorrowful. They would promise you anything, just to get some sleep. When they woke up it was; the attitude "It's not any of your business, I'm grown."

Another occurrence started when Thomas had taken my Automatic Teller Machine, (ATM) card, and had successfully taken out one hundred dollars. I had to go take the money out of the bank, and letting the bank personnel know that he had stolen it. I was driving down the road when I saw Thomas. I called him and he looked so pitiful that I wanted to hold him in my arms and protect him. He didn't run, as a matter of fact, he slowly came toward me; afraid of what I knew, and what I would do to him. Getting in the car, he tried to explain to me why he did it, and why he was never going to do it again. "I'm not going to do this again. I don't know why I stole your ATM card mom, but I swear I'm never going to do crack again." He was so apologetic, and I was so happy to hear that he was through with this drug. I just wanted to take him in my arms but what I did was take him home with me.

As I put away the groceries I heard the news flash announce a thunderstorm alert. I called, "Thomas could you go to the school to pick up Melissa, it's about to rain." I don't know what I was thinking, as I left Thomas in the room with my purse, which carried five hundred dollars. Forgetting all about his drug problem, I quickly made it our problem, as I gave him the keys to our van. I didn't think anything else about it. I was cooking dinner so I lost track of time until Melissa walked in the front door soaking wet.

I asked, "Where's Thomas?" She screamed, "Why didn't someone pick me up? I'm soaking wet. I haven't seen Thomas." It flashed across my mind at that moment to check my wallet. The wallet I had just placed five hundred dollars in at the bank. Need I say it was empty? I had taken it out of the bank so Thomas couldn't take it out with the ATM card, and then I gave the rest to him in cash. But it was worse even than that. He had also taken my van. It was a 1995, Dodge conversion van. What to do, what to do?

I felt so foolish. I realized that this is what crack does to the non-user. We have to be alert at all times when dealing with the crack addict. There's an old saying about crack users. Question: "When do you know when a crack head is lying?" Answer: "When their lips are moving," I learned a lot through the next fifth teen years. Not too long after the incident with Thomas, Tony decided to take off after work again; when he didn't come home after work. I knew he went on a binge. I had not gotten even a phone call from him in three days. I told him, after he returned three days later, "Tony, this is not going to work.

You need to get a place of your own. I can't have you and Thomas on my back. You, and Thomas are trying to kill me; you need to move immediately." This is what I told him and so he left to get his own apartment across town. A few weeks after Tony left, Thomas was again in need at my door. He had been on the streets a couple of weeks, so of course he was dirty, needing a change of clothes but above all, he needed a bath. My son and I talked a while, when I told him I would help him get an apartment. I couldn't trust him in my home, but I was still his mother. I didn't want him to do badly. I again did something that only a mother understood; maybe not every mother. I co-signed for his apartment. I made the first and last month rent, as well as the deposit. It was fun watching Thomas; looking throughout the apartment we decided on. I even bought him some groceries.

About a week after he moved into his apartment, Thomas showed up at my house saying, "I'm just visiting so I could talk to someone." I told him, "You don't need an excuse; you know it's always nice to see you darling." Thomas indicated that he had a job working for the neighborhood Walgreens. He, as usually, was very excited about his new job. I hesitated when he said he worked at the cashier position. "Too close to money," is what I was thinking, and I told him as much. He assured me it wasn't like that. He said, "Why can't you just be happy for me? Leave the past alone and stop preaching about the past, all the time?" I left it alone, after I said, "History teaches us that we learn by our mistakes. I really don't understand why you can't see that," and then I let it go. He was grown so he needed to learn from his own mistakes.

Later that night, about 2:00 AM in the morning, I answered the phone. It was the store manager of the neighborhood Walgreens, asking me, "Mrs. Smith, do you know the whereabouts of your son?" He continued, "It seems, he took his break at midnight, and he has not returned back from break. When we checked the register the money was gone, and so is he." I told him "Sir, I'm sure that Thomas will not be coming back. He is on that stuff they call "crack." I am so sorry. Can you tell me how much it will cost to keep you from calling the law?" He told me, I paid him, and I prayed that this was the last time I would hear about it. I went to Thomas' apartment manager, which was kind enough to cut up his lease as long as she could keep the application fee, and the security deposit.

In the meantime, by this time Tony and I had gotten back together it was good for a while. Then one day it was Tony's pay day, so of course, Tony had disappeared after work. He didn't call or anything for three days. When he returned he admitted that he had gone out, and used crack again. He also owed the dealer five hundred dollars. Since Tony had a good job, the dealers didn't hesitate to extend him credit. I tried to reason with Tony that our bills should come first, and the dealers were not his friend. One day I was arguing with him because he is giving the dealers money again that we needed to pay our bills, and he told me, "I know they're not my friends. I did not give the dealer anything." He stated rather smartly, "I bought a commodity."

I was so turned off by his attitude, "You are hopelessly hooked on the drug, and you are making no sense at all." It was bad enough that my husband and son were addicted to this drug. One day my brothers who came down from Milwaukee were living with me. I am all for family but soon I discovered they were also using crack. It disappointed me when Chris arrived, only to tell me, upon his arrival, "Sis, I have been taking crack and I'm trying to get off the drug." Was I the only sane person left in America? I was beginning to feel like a crack magnet, and a door mat.

You're Out of the Army Now; 1999

1999 found Bill Gates personal fortune in excess of *"one hundred billion dollars,[217]"* due to the increased value of Microsoft stock, Microsoft released *"Windows 98 (Second Edition),[218]" "Apple Computer[219]"* released the first *"iBook,[220]"* the *"first Laptop designed[221]"* specifically for average consumers, Apple Computer released the "Power Macintosh G4,222" the *"Columbine High School massacre;[223]"* two Littleton, Colorado teenagers, Eric Harris, and Dylan Klebold, opened fire on their teachers, and classmates, killing twelve students, and one teacher, and then themselves." *"Benjamin Nathaniel Smith[224]"* began a three day killing spree targeting racial and ethnic minorities in Illinois, and Indiana, *"Star Wars Episode I; the Phantom Menace[225]"* was released in theaters. It became the highest grossing Star Wars film. *"Governor George W. Bush[226]"* announced he would seek the Republican Party nomination for President of the United States, the *"World population[227]"* reached six billion people, according to the United Nations, and I retired out of the military after twenty two years of service.

It was March 1999; I was sitting in my home office when I got a phone call from my sister Paula, (nine months my senior). She was crying uncontrollably. I repeatedly asked her over and over, "Paula what is wrong?" I finally piece together what she was trying to tell me. I already knew that Monica was going to the hospital, since I spoke to her the previous week, to have a simple procedure. Monica had said, "There is no reason to worry. If something unusual does happen, Aunt Donna will call you to let you know."

Paula told me, through her tears that Monica had been in surgery longer than the doctors had expected. Paula said, "Sissy, you've got to get here. I don't know what to do. I've never had to go through anything like this. I have no one to talk to or help me get through this. The doctors don't expect her to live. They have her on a respirator but they only give her a couple of days to survive…"

I told Thomas, Melissa, Deidra, and Tony what Paula had told me. Tony agreed with me that I needed to go to Milwaukee, but he couldn't since he had to work. He took me to the bus station; Deidra picked me up at the Atlanta Bus Station that night. I had a flight to Milwaukee, that following morning to take me to the Atlanta Airport. Once at the Milwaukee Airport, I rented a car and went to Paula's house to get directions. When I arrived at Paula's house I had told her I would wait for her to wash a load of clothes before going to Monica's house, so she would have something to wear.

As I was entering Paula's apartment she was telling me, "Monica's sons are picking her up to take her home now." This is where I told myself, "There is something wrong about this. Monica's sons didn't have a car, so what were they going to take her home in; a bus, or a cab maybe? If Monica was on life support yesterday, how was she going home today?" I said, "Well I'll go to Monica's house to see her there." Paula interjected, "I don't think that is a good idea.

When I told Monica you were coming, her reaction was, "That hussy better not grace my door-step. She didn't even call the hospital to see how I was doing." Paula continued, "She also said she didn't want to see you. Something about an argument you two had and something else about she wasn't talking to you, so if you came to her house she was going to kick your ass." But with this being said, I told her, "Paula, get a ride with Patrick (Patrick was her son). I need to squash whatever this is. I'll see you when you get there."

The phone rang, and Paula was busy in the laundry room so I answered it. It was my Aunt Donna, "Hello Aunt Donna, this is Sissy, I just got here." Aunt Donna said, "Why are you and Monica acting like this? You know ya'll need to stop acting like this." I continued, "Auntie, I have no idea what you mean about "acting like this," I just arrived. I am on my way to see Monica. If she is upset with me, she needs to tell me." Aunt Donna stated, "That is fine baby, but don't you two get to fighting down there. Okay?" I said, "Auntie, you know me.

There isn't gonna be no fighting, I love all my blood relatives too much for that; although I am beginning to believe my family watches too much "Jerry Springer." We both laughed at this. "That's why I'm going over to Monica's house now. I need to make sure she is okay as well. That's why I'm here. I need to go now Auntie, I'll tell Paula you called, okay?" Aunt Donna also said good bye. After I called down to the laundry room to tell Paula of Auntie's phone call, I left. Something else didn't get pass me; I wondered why Aunt Donna thought Monica, and I were fighting. I arrived at Monica's, and she was all smiles when I got there. She put her arms around me, and seemed genuinely surprised by my presence. We had a lot to talk, and laugh about so I didn't have to mention anything about Paula's drama. I waited until Paula, and Patrick arrived, and was seated before I mentioned what Paula had said. "Paula, why did you call me crying, talking about what the doctor had said about Monica not having long to live. How she was on the life support system, and how you were afraid because the doctors said that Monica was going to die, overnight."

Paula looked at Monica than me, not knowing how much Monica knew. Monica broke the silence when she asked, "What are ya'll talking about?" Paula said with laughter in her voice, "Yeah, I said it; I wanted to see my baby sister. So I lied, and I'd do it again." I said to Paula, "Yeah, well I guess you're going to pay my bills for getting here with your social security check you get every month." Monica asked, "Paula, what have you done this time? I knew you loved to keep shit going, but this time I think you've gone too far. How could you fix your mouth to tell Sissy that I was on my death bed? You never even came to the hospital to see me." "That isn't all," I continued, "she thought I was going to find out she was lying, so she told me, if I came over here, you were going to kick my ass." We both thought that was funny, because we both knew that I respected Monica's position in our family chain.

She was older than me. I also respected how she carried herself in everything she did. We also each believed we could beat the other, even though we never fought. I told Paula, "Trust is something that takes time to earn, but it only takes a few minutes to lose. Paula, you are still my sister, but if you ever tell me something or someone needs my presence, you better get a co-signer." I stayed in Milwaukee at Monica's the first three days. I knew how Monica felt about my brothers. It came very close to hate. I never understood it but I accepted it. I didn't want an argument, so I waited until about eight o'clock the night before to mention that I was going to my parent's home to visit my brothers for a day. I didn't wait for an answered.

I went upstairs to sleep. The next morning I woke up to a loud telephone conversation coming from my sister, Monica to, I'm sure was my sister Paula. Monica was saying, "...she don't pick up after herself, she hasn't washed a dish since she's been here. Yeah, yeah!!! That's right." She continued, "She doesn't want to go anywhere, or do anything, all she wants to do is lie around on the couch and watch television." I was flabbergasted to overhear this bogus account of my character. From the first day I arrived, I had tried to wash dishes, cleaned up after myself, and make up the bed I was sleeping on. She would jump up, and take the dishes to clean them. When I tried to wash, and fold the bedding I used, to show my appreciation of her hospitality. No matter what it was she would tell me, "Its fine, go sit down, it will go faster if I do it."

As far as the movies, she kept saying it was too hot outside or she just didn't feel up to going anywhere, and she kept showing me all the movies she had saved. As I got out of the bed, I chose to take the bed covers off the bed I had been sleeping on. I brought them downstairs, and put them into the dirty cloths hamper. I don't know whether she thought I overheard the telephone call but I calmly said my goodbyes with no manner of, hysterics, and drove to my brothers' house. I expected a more serious departure. I was glad there wasn't one. I hated drama.

Until Love We Do Part; 2002

I continued to have even more complications with Tony, and his addiction to crack. When he wasn't doing crack he would indulge in liquor or beer, even though he rarely looked or acted intoxicated. I think I heard it from everyone; my medical doctor, whom I shared with Tony, my psychiatrist, my sisters, my daughters, and of course my psychoanalyst. They all wanted me to leave him. I just couldn't bring myself to do it. I admit it hurt sometimes; especially when Tony would disappear, or when we didn't have enough money to make ends meet, but he was my best friend. As we grew older we witnessed our other friends pass away for various reasons.

We always knew we could depend on each other. We were each other's best friend. When he wasn't indulging in crack, he was the sweetest man. He was gentle and kind. He never hit me or denied me anything within his realm of control that is. I knew he would do anything for me; except, stop smoking crack. As I said, when he did indulge, he would disappear for days, leaving me to worry alone. When he did return, all he wanted to do was sleep. He would be out for all of that day after he returned. He was very apologetic and would beat himself up before he went to bed. He knew that he shouldn't do crack. Besides the large amount of money he was wasting, it was bad for his health and he could get arrested.

Most of the time, after he did crack, or he ran out of credit, he would be located in some worn out vacant house on the poorer side of town. The dealers had little respect for him, not only because he was hooked and they weren't; the drug dealers had better sense than to use their own product. They also made fun of him because they were young men, and he was up there in age. When an addict was of no use (the money ran out), they had to leave the drug house. It seemed that with all this going on Tony, Thomas, and my brothers were hopelessly hooked, and would keep going back.

Thomas was gone for days; he was on another binge. When he returned home I said, "Thomas, this is not going to work. You need to get a place of your own. I can't have you and Tony on my back. I'm going to get you an apartment, but you need to get a job, as soon as possible so you can take over the rent, and utilities." So this is what I did. It was fun watching Thomas as he look over the apartment we decided on. I even bought him some groceries. About a week after he moved into his apartment, Thomas showed up at my house saying, "I'm just visiting so I could talk to someone." I told him, "You know it's always nice to see you darling."

I know I should have known from his pass actions, but I took my eyes off of him. Taking my guard down gave him an opportunity to take off with my van. I wasn't mad; I just wanted my van back. I believed by this time, the pain was embedded deep inside of my heart. When Thomas took my van, this time I called the police. It just so happened that this night was the night he, and another man committed a robbery to the neighborhood Walgreens that Thomas had worked at a couple of weeks earlier. Thomas had earlier lent the van to a crack dealer. Since I had called the Sherriff Department, they identified the van, pulled it over, and arrested his crack dealer, and his wife. Thomas went to jail, and I got my van back.

As I heard it from Thomas, "The man I was with was just someone I spoke to on the street. I took him to my place. When we ran out of booze, we left the apartment. I thought we were going to get some more booze." He continued the story with excitement in his gestures, "Then this guy told me to steal from the same Walgreens I had worked at just a couple of weeks ago. Mom, you remember, the one? I was fired because I stole from the cash register, and then went on break, never to be seen again. I tried to reason with the guy, telling him I use to work here, but he smiled at me, pulled out a gun, and told me to get out of his car, go into the store, and come out with the money.

Since I knew where the button was to call the police, I stood in front of the guy at the register and gestured for him to push the button. I knew he was afraid about now but he had no idea how afraid I was. I did everything but jumped over the counter, and push the damn button myself. He finally pushed the button. I grabbed a few dollars, to make it look good, but I was in no hurry to go back to that car with that fool waiting with the gun. I heard the sirens getting close so instead of going to the car, I turned right instead of left, and tried to get away from both that fool and the police."

It was about now that I remembered the saying… "How do you know when a crack head is lying?" Answer, "When their lips are moving." I continued to love my son. I learned a lot about the prison system thanks to my son. I would go to visit him every Wednesday, in the prison, which was a chore. No matter whether you come early or late, you are going to wait. You see people lined up along the wall, sitting; standing, some on the floor, or some brought portable chairs with them. If you are visiting your loved ones, you need to have a picture I.D. If you leave money it had to be a money order or cashier check. Most of the people visiting the prisoners were females; mothers, daughters, sisters, wives, and lovers.

It's at least a two hour wait but you can only see them for fifteen minutes. The guards treated the visitors as if they committed a crime. The crime was; loving, caring or just fraternize with the prisoners. Then there is the court system. That is another totally different world. The court assigns a lawyer that doesn't really care what happens to the convict. The court would allow you to talk to the convict briefly but only to convince the convict to plead guilty. The judge puts out the charges, than tells the convict what he needs to pay and do after the trial.

There is an organization called TASC. The organization is to help the convict to recover from the drugs. They do this by assigning a color to the convict. Each convict has to call in daily to find out the color that is being tested, through the use of a Urinalysis. If they come up positive, the convict's parole or probation can be revoked. They just want you to pay the enrollment fees. The convict is also assigned a probation or parole officer. The convict also has to pay them fees monthly. When the convict doesn't have a job, due to no fault of the convict, the convict/addict very easily goes right back into the life of addiction.

Thomas was the only kind of crack user in my environment that also got mixed up with the judicial system. But he was also the only one that would steal from his own home. My psychologist tells me he is a sociopath. I really didn't know what to do about him. It was hard for me to take advice from Tony in this area since he also was addicted to crack. I wanted to stand by, not only Thomas but especially Tony. Thomas was my son but Tony was my husband. Sometimes I really believed the only reason Tony would tell me to turn my back on Thomas, was because it left more money for him to use rather then, "to allow Thomas to grow," as he would tell me. I also felt to him it meant it left me alone to deal with just his tribulations.

Thomas had gotten so bad with his addiction that we, Melissa and I, would cry for him. We would talk about him being one of the crack addicts that would smoke in vacant houses, eating out of trash cans, and pan handling downtown to get money to buy more crack. When we saw him on the street, or when he returned to our house to beg for money to eat, even though we knew he was going to use the money to buy more crack. He had lost so much weight and his clothes were so dirty. We were even afraid of him, as well as for him. We didn't know what he was capable of.

Crack gets Stronger/I Get Weaker; 2005

It was 2005, when *"Hurricane Katrina,*[228]*"* named by the Atlantic hurricane season, became the costliest natural disaster, as well as, one of the five deadliest hurricanes in the history of the United States, George W. Bush was inaugurated in Washington, D.C. for his second term as the *"forty-third President of the United States,*[229]*"* North Korea announced they possessed *"nuclear weapons*[230]*"* as a protection against the hostility it felt from the United States. One night Thomas came to my home really down. It was Christmas Eve; Tony was at work, so he was not home.

I wanted to let Thomas in, but honestly Melissa and I were both afraid of what he might do. Would Thomas just steal something or would he ever physically hurt one of us. Thomas begged us for over an hour, with real tears in his eyes. He had been on the streets for a couple of weeks and it was cold outside. Thomas swore that he wouldn't take anything, but we had heard this so many times before. I just couldn't trust him. I probably would have done it if it was just me, but I was worried about Melissa. Thomas asked if he could stay in the shed, or even just sleep in the van. I didn't think that was a good idea.

Finally I decided that if he would be willing I would be able to sleep with him in the house if I tied him to the bed, and had the door to the bedroom locked from my side. He agreed with this so that is how Melissa and I spent Christmas Eve with Thomas. This was truly not my ideal family Christmas. Thomas would steal from his own family to get his drugs, not like Tony. Tony was another style of addict. He was known as a "functional addict." He had a good job that the drug dealers knew about.

They loved to see him coming because when he would show up everyone got high. Tony would break out his paycheck and party until it was gone. Then he would keep getting high when the money was gone so when he left the party he still owed the dealers hundreds of dollars. I would beg Tony to stop this ritual he had gotten into. It went something like this. He would work for a little less than two weeks. Since he got paid every other Thursdays, that meant he was regular for about two weeks. Then every other week, around Wednesday, he would "*fade to black*" as the saying goes. It was around this time that his body started to crave the drugs. By Wednesday night, when he would get off work, he always failed to make it home. In the meantime I was at home on the internet waiting for his check to get deposited. I would trace when he would make that first debit. I always knew where he was by the location he debited from. Once I saw the activity in the bank account start, I would know that he wasn't coming home.

I would call him on his cell phone, which he always answered; at least until it ran out of battery life. He would tell me he was on his way home, but two, three hours later he was still out there. I would transfer the rest of our money into an account he couldn't access. Once he couldn't get any more money or credit from the dealers, he would sit in the deserted crack houses feeling sorry for his pitiful self, and for what he had done. Then he would come home, only for the lost of nowhere else to go. Once he returned home he would be so depressed he would cry and say he would do anything to stop using crack.

He would disappear for at least three days. It got so bad that I would have to try several tactics to get at least some of the money to pay a few of the bills. Once he woke up, the promises he made the day before were not even worth discussing. He swore he had this drug under control, so I was not to worry. He would also come up with the excuses that he would tell his job why he was late or absent, depending on the recovery time. He would then go back to work like nothing happened.

The biggest problem in the house was Thomas; he not only got high a lot more than the others, he would steal from us or anyone to do so. Eventually Tony and I felt like a supply warehouse. He would steal it and we would replace it. He would steal jewelry, cell phones, cars or anything negotiable. There was a saying, "Anyone that will steal from their mother will steal from anyone." And he did. Thomas' ability to keep a job was a joke. He had a jovial personality, when he was sober; so charming and humorous that you trusted him right off.

People would hire him and give him lots of responsibilities. One time his employer liked him so much, when he discovered Thomas didn't have a ride, he gave him a car. He not only failed to show up after he got a paycheck, he also gave away the car. He would always disappoint his benefactors by stealing their money, giving away property, or just disappearing for days at a time. The drama was especially around paydays. It became apparent that Thomas could not have money or some other form of collateral, and transportation at the same time. He would always get high. When I returned from Korea to Alabama, I learned how bad my son's addiction to crack was. Basically, if the urge for crack hit him, he had to get some; even if it meant trading away his or someone else's car, cell phone, camcorders, or whatever. I actually had to pay thirty-five dollars to a drug dealer to get my car back after Thomas sold it for thirty five dollars of crack.

What was I thinking that would keep me in this life? The hell if I knew. Some days I would pray that one day this all would stop. Most days I was just so busy trying to get through the episode. Being very spiritual, I knew that if I kept my faith someday this too would pass. I loved my family and I could never put my finger on when this all started. Recently I had acquired an empty nest, with Melissa graduating out of high school and going off to college.

The children grew up and moved out and I retired from the military relatively around the same time. Tony and I have moved all our real living down to the first floor since we don't need all this space. I was proud when my Melissa graduated and went to college; it also hit me like a ton of bricks. I had already retired out of the military. It slowly dawned on me that all of my children were gone from my arms. I realized that I had what they called an *"empty nest."* I felt relief in a way, since now I didn't have to feel I was hurting my children by holding on to Tony.

When he disappeared on one of his binges I didn't have to feel fear and shame until he returned. Fear because I had no idea where he was or if he was even alive. Shame because I knew I would take him back. I also felt I no longer had a life. I'm not sure when I started to realize that I was not alone. I wasn't alone at home, in my yard, looking around at my garden. It was then that I realized that I wasn't alone and the Lord was not finished with me. I still had a mission in me, a purpose in life.

I don't know, maybe that is when I started volunteering at the Veteran's Administration Hospital. I also started going to college; first residential, and then on-line. I felt alive when I was helping people, and I knew I had something more to give. I didn't feel it was about going to school and getting passing grades so you could get a better job. My character is made up to believe that what is the point of doing something, unless you do your best? It is always good to do the best you can, or don't do it at all. I also believe it's about getting up every morning, and doing something worthwhile that gives a person a purpose in life. I have found the warmth of my blood running through my body; it lets me know I'm alive. Every day I wake up it is another beautiful day. A day I feel is a gift from the Lord. I have another chance to serve my Lord.

Because I know how much I love myself. Many times I would ask myself if there was something I could have done differently. But I know we cannot go back in time. What we did is final. These are the times I had to remember how I was a member of a family of twelve children. My mother and father treated us all the same. They were not responsible for the way we turned out. They did the best they could in raising us. Of those twelve children I went in a different direction with my life. Why would I feel any other way for my children?

There were the times I would want to take my life in another direction. I just wanted to run away to start a different life; with Melissa graduating out of high school and going off to college. I sometimes believe that this is where my bipolar started; the children grew up and moved out, and I retired from the military around the same time. Wouldn't you know it; we finally earned enough to buy a tri-level home but now nobody is around to enjoy it. I had begun to have numerous bouts of depression and frequent mood swings when I was diagnosed as being bi-polar.

Cancer Thrives on Stress; 2006

It was in 2006 that North Korea claimed to have conducted its first-ever nuclear test, *"South Korean's Ban Ki-moon[231]"* was elected as the new Secretary-General of the United Nations, the establishment of the *"Islamic State of Iraq[232]"* was declared, former president of *"Iraq, Saddam Hussein[233]"* was sentenced to death by hanging by the *"Iraqi Special Tribunal.[234]"* I have found the warmth of my blood running through my body lets me know I'm alive. Every day I wake up is another wonderful, beautiful day. A day I feel is a gift from the Lord. I have another chance to serve him.

I know why I continue with my sobriety. It is difficult, since it seems that everyone else is intoxicated on something or other; if not by alcohol, than by other drugs. Everyone in my environment feels there is nothing wrong with smoking marijuana. An increasing number of them feel their use of crack should be acceptable. I promised myself that I would not indulge in intoxicants while I was in the military. Once I retired from the army, I could have easily started up again, but I just felt if it wasn't broke, why fix it.

I remembered how much I disliked myself when I drank alcohol. I didn't lose respect for others that indulged in mind altering substances; that was their decision to tolerate. It just wasn't good for me. I felt it would be insane to go back to using drugs or alcohol. Especially when I witnessed the transitions people that I loved went through while indulging in the world of intoxicants. My biggest fear hadn't happened yet. That being me going back into the world of the drinking and smoking; and using anything to get high on.

The insanity continued to play out; Tony going back and forth in the world of crack, and my worrying about him. He would be fine for a couple of weeks; until he got paid every two weeks. He became what I wanted to believe his true self; when he wasn't using crack. But around payday he would disappear. He didn't come home from work. He was in his other world; the crack world. I was not accepted or even welcome in that world. I wouldn't know where he was, or when he would return. I could track his whereabouts by getting on the internet. I could see where he debited our account every time he went back to get more money to get more crack.

I would call his cell phone, and he would answer it. He would give his word that he was on his way home. Two or three hours later he still wouldn't return home. He would spend hundreds of dollars on crack. I would go withdraw the remaining money from the bank. Once he couldn't get money from the bank, he would return home. Upon his return, he would be apologetic and self loading. He would swear he would never do it again as he told me how many hundreds of dollars he owed the drug dealers. He would always insist that he had to pay the drug dealers their money, before we paid the bills.

Even though I tried to convince him this was just another way he ensued his account was cleared so he would be welcomed back by the drug dealers. He swore this was not the case. The next pay period would find him missing again. It would take him longer to recover with each episode. It seemed his body grew weaker as he grew older. Sometimes, when he returned, he would sleep for an entire day, sometimes two days. He lost weight, and although he is usually very energetic, he didn't find any interest in doing chores around the house or socializing with me or others.

I would sometimes make attempts to wake him, but his sleep was sound. Sometimes when he was asleep in our bed, I could feel how restless he really was. He would be fighting in his sleep talking, and waving his arms around; I would worry about him hitting me while we slept. He talks in his sleep but it never made sense. It was unintelligible noises that only proved how much the drug was physically and emotionally affecting him. In addition to Tony's addiction, two of my brothers were now also residing in my home. They had been using crack in Milwaukee but they felt if they moved to a different state they could beat the drug.

They had a lot of respect for me (or so they said to my face), so if they were using, they didn't do it around me. This is what I wanted to believe, so that is why they let me see. They never got high in my presence, or with each other. When I took them around to get jobs, and they attained employment, they didn't want to pay for rent or food. They would disappear during pay days and when they returned, they were broke. They didn't even have cigarettes and I didn't smoke so I would get irritated when they would ask me for cigarettes. Need I say they were jobless again so here we were at the beginning? The stress would affect me when I felt unappreciated. I'm really not brainless. I knew the real insanity of this is doing what you've been doing and expecting a different outcome.

Yet even with all these problems it seemed I kept my life seemingly separate from their crack-filled existence. This was until I was diagnosed with cancer; breast cancer to be exact. I actually thought since I didn't indulge in drugs, it was okay in allowing the others in my life to act a fool. It seemed as if the joke was on me. I was being penalized for supporting drug abusers. I realized later that I was trying to make them want to live in my lifestyle; the lifestyle that I had come to know. Once I had been diagnosis with cancer I felt it was necessary to be alone with my thoughts. I was so perplexed about this new direction my life had taken. I isolated myself in a section of my home. I just wanted to be alone to think. I needed to get closer to my Lord.

As I quietly meditated in the dark; no television or music, I started to hear my own thoughts. They were clearly assisting me to make sense out of these circumstances. I mentally envisioned a horse-race track. The horses were lined up to depart the gate. It seemed as though the horses were ready to go but the gate would not open. This vision was clear. I was the gate and the horses represented my relatives. Whenever the Lord placed tribulations in their path, I would fix it. I was keeping the gate closed, just as I was, undeniably, keeping my family from their rewards. I heard my voice telling me, "I love you. When did I ask for your help in this manner? I have rewarded you for the decisions you've made in your life. I have given you tests to overcome, and as you passed each tribulation, I have rewarded you with a better lifestyle. The lifestyle you enjoy is my way of ensuring you can continue on future endeavors. I love you Sissy, but what made you think I loved them any less?"

That is why I still believe the Lord will never give us more than we can handle. My home and the respect others have for me are my "spoils of war," as I like to call them. It was very clear when the Lord spoke to me, I knew the Lord, who was there for me in every way, was also there for each of my relatives. The Lord was also giving them tribulations to overcome. How was he to know whether they were ready for the next step in life if I wouldn't let them out of the gate? I was so busy saving them; I didn't realize that the Lord wanted them to save themselves. I began to visualize the Lord saying, "When did I ask for your assistance. You are really not helping these people in the manner you are doing." I said to my Lord; "Please don't take me away like this. I see your point and I swear I will get out of your way."

I felt enlightened and relieved. I knew that Tony was my soul-mate, given to me by the Lord. If there is any fixing of him; it will be repaired by the Lord. I left my room to tell my brothers and Thomas what I felt I had say. "You guys have to find somewhere else to go during the hours of nine to five, Monday through Friday. You don't have to go looking for a job or move out, but you do have to leave my home during those hours.

I don't need a babysitter nor do I want you to do the landscaping around my house. Tony has a job, he's paying the bills and I will not have him take care of grown men. We also need to be alone sometimes." I felt this was what I should tell them. It was as if a heavy weight had somehow lifted off me. I knew that once I made that statement the Lord would do the rest. It must have been perfect because that was on a Saturday and the following Monday my son and two brothers were no longer in my house.

I don't know what happened, but I knew my Lord was watching over them, and I really didn't care. I was just happy that they no longer were around to make me feel that I was standing in God's way. That following week, after I had surgery, the results of the pathologist came in. It was an eight percent chance of the cancer coming back and I didn't have to have chemotherapy or radiation treatments. I believed my Lord heard my prayers. The relatives' absence didn't last forever but it was a good while before they returned. In the scheme of a lifetime, it was only a few months, but they at least knew Tony and I didn't want them to stay in our home forever. I know my words might hurt some;

even surprise others, but I felt the telling of my story can, or even will be of use to others depended on me telling it as I lived it. It has already been therapeutic for me to tell it just as it happened. I'm not sure how the subsequent episodes in my life will unfold, but I'm sure I will entitle the next book, "As the Stomach Churns" and I know it will be a block buster.

Endnotes

1. http://www.thepeoplehistory.com/1951.html
2. http://www.youtube.com/watch?v=lrI7dVj90zs
3. http://sportsthenandnow.com/tag/1951-national-league-pennant/
4. http://www.enotes.com/catcher-in-the-rye/
5. http://www.fiftiesweb.com/lucy.htm
6. http://www.enotes.com/authors/tennessee-williams
7. http://www.whitehouse.gov/about/presidents/harrystruman/
8. http://www.history.army.mil/faq/mac_bio.htm
9. http://armed-services.senate.gov/
10. http://foreign.senate.gov/
11. http://victory1945.rt.com/films/europe-spring-1945-europe/
12. http://www.fda.gov/
13. http://uktv.co.uk/yesterday/homepage/sid/5436
14. http://www.aretha-franklin.com/bio.htm
15. http://www.thebeatles.com/
16. http://www.imdb.com/title/tt0040053/
17. http://www.historyplace.com/unitedstates/vietnam/index-1969.html
18. http://www.tv.com/star-trek/show/633/summary.html
19. http://www.marxist.com/1968/
20. http://www.last.fm/music/Frank+Sinatra
21. http://nobelprize.org/nobel_prizes/peace/laureates/1964/king-bio.html
22. http://www.uic.edu/orgs/cwluherstory/Jofreeman/photos/McCarthy.html
23. http://www.whitehouse.gov/about/presidents/lyndonbjohnson

24. http://www.spartacus.schoolnet.co.uk/USAkennedyR.htm
25. http://www.stonewallvets.org/DianaRoss.htm
26. http://www.pbs.org/battlefieldvietnam/guerrilla/index.html
27. http://www.infoplease.com/ipa/A0760621.html#axzz0zMpWEV87
28. http://www.trutv.com/library/crime/terrorists_spies/assassins/ray/1.html
29. http://www.youtube.com/watch?v=pb0bV5CPIUM
30. http://www.findadeath.com/Deceased/g/Garland,Judy/judy_garland.htm
31. http://history1900s.about.com/od/1960s/p/charlesmanson.htm
32. http://www.findadeath.com/Deceased/t/tate/tate_murders.htm
33. http://newyork.mets.mlb.com/index.jsp?c_id=nym
34. http://topics.nytimes.com/topics/reference/timestopics/subjects/s/sesame_ street/index.html
35. http://www2.cddc.vt.edu/marxists/history/usa/workers/black-panthers/index.htm
36. http://www.democracynow.org/2009/12/4/the_assassination_of_fred_hampton_how
37. http://health.howstuffworks.com/diseases-conditions/infectious/aids.htm
38. http://www.dwightdeisenhower.com/biodde.html
39. http://www.songfacts.com/detail.php?id=247
40. http://www.imdb.com/title/tt0066626/
41. http://www.intel.com/p/en_US/business/design
42. http://www.wireclub.com/
43. http://www.youtube.com/watch?v=AVV- OGGEa6A
44. http://www.brainyhistory.com/events/1971/march_1_1971_140184.html
45. http://www.cnlawrence.com/papers/busing.pdf
46. http://www.druglibrary.org/schaffer/library/studies/nc/nc2b_10.htm
47. http://barbra-archives.com/record/albums/barbra_joan_streisand.html
48. http://www.filmsite.org/sple.html
49. http://lyricsplayground.com/alpha/songs/b/breakuptomakeup.shtml
50. http://www.watergate.info/
51. http://www.boxing-memorabilia.com/bioforeman.htm

52. http://www.astronautix.com/flights/skylab4.htm
53. http://www.digitalhistory.uh.edu/modules/vietnam/index.cfm
54. http://www.microsoft.com/presspass/exec/billg/
55. http://www.apple.com/
56. http://web.mit.edu/invent/iow/apple.html
57. http://www.whitehouse.gov/about/presidents/jimmycarter/
58. http://www.whitehouse.gov/about/presidents/geraldford
59. http://www.kirjasto.sci.fi/ahaley.htm
60. http://apple2history.org/
61. http://www.elvis.com/elvisology/bio/elvis_overview.asp
62. http://www.nndb.com/people/278/000025203/
63. http://www.marx-brothers.org/biography/marxes.htm
64. http://www.ssa.gov/pubs/10101.html
65. http://www.fns.usda.gov/snap/rules/Legislation/history/PL_95-113.htm
66. http://www.baseball-reference.com/players/j/jacksre01.shtml
67. http://www.imdb.com/title/tt0076759/
68. http://www.answers.com/topic/the-bee-gees
69. http://www.answers.com/topic/john-travolta
70. http://www.answers.com/topic/olivia-newton-john
71. http://www.answers.com/topic/commodores
72. http://www-chaos.umd.edu/history/prc.html
73. http://www.infoplease.com/biography/var/pattyhearst.html
74. http://www.ibiblio.org/sullivan/bios/Sadat-bio.html
75. http://www.jewishvirtuallibrary.org/jsource/biography/begin.html
76. http://www.encyclopedia.com/topic/Ahmad_Hasan_al-Bakr.aspx
77. http://www.answers.com/topic/saddam-hussein
78. http://www.queermusicheritage.us/march79.html
79. http://www.answers.com/topic/edward-m-ted-kennedy
80. http://www.answers.com/topic/tehran
81. http://www.answers.com/topic/executive-order-12170
82. http://www.iranian.com/
83. http://www.answers.com/topic/ruhollah-khomeini
84. http://www.answers.com/topic/uniform-code-of-military-justice
85. http://www.nizamcanvas.com/gpt.htm
86. http://www.1campingtent.com/the-a-tent-or-pup-tent.htm
87. http://www.autofuelstc.com/autofuelstc/pa/Start_Here.html

88. http://encyclopedia2.thefreedictionary. com/Mogas
89. http://www.prescriptiondrug- info.com/topics/x112/
90. http://www.mapsofworld.com/olympics/moscow-ussr-1980-
     olympic-games.html
91. http://www.uscatholic.org/oscar_romero
92. http://www.geographia.com/bahamas/bsssin01.htm
93. http://www.helis.com/featured/eagle_claw.php
94. http://www.miamibeach411.com/news/index.php?/news/
     comments/mcduffie - riots/
95. http://www.starwars.com/movies/episode-v/
96. http://pacman.com/en/
97. http://www.cnn.com/
98. http://www.anc.org.za/
99. http://nobelprize.org/nobel_prizes/peace/laureates/1993/
     mandela-bio.html
100. http://www.archives.gov/federal- register/codification/
     proclamations/04771.html
101. http://www.militaryspot.com/resources/item/military_draft
102. http://www.guidetorussia.com/russia-afghanistan.asp
103. http://www.americanrhetoric.com/speeches/tedkennedy1980dnc.
     htm
104. http://www.facebook.com/pages/United-States-presidential-
     election-1980/143080672371738
105. http://www.u-s-history.com/pages/h2021.html
106. http://www.ultimatedallas.com/movie/
107. http://www.infoplease.com/ipa/A0760624.html
108. http://americanhistory.about.com/od/ronaldreagan/p/preagan.
     htm
109. http://manhattan.ny1.com/content/features/10287/january-20th-
     in-nyc-history
110. http://www.cbsnews.com/stories/2009/07/17/eveningnews/
     main5170556.shtml
111. http://www.cdc.gov/
112. http://www.cdc.gov/mmwr/preview/mmwrhtml/mm5021a2.htm
113. http://www.carpenoctem.tv/killers/williams.html
114. http://www.simonandgarfunkel.com/
115. http://www.centralpark.com/pages/activities/concerts.html
116. http://www.historylink.org/index.cfm?DisplayPage=output.
     cfm&file_id=382

117. http://www.epa.gov/
118. http://www.cqs.com/edioxin.htm
119. http://www.legendsofamerica.com/mo-timesbeach.html
120. http://www.house.gov/
121. http://www.asianamericanmedia.org/jainternment/
122. http://www.coldwar.org/articles/80s/SDI-StarWars.asp
123. http://www.lucidcafe.com/library/96may/ride.html
124. http://phoenix.about.com/od/attractionsandevents/u/ ThingsToDoInPhoenix.htm
125. http://www.ukpolitical.info/1983.htm
126. http://www.gps.gov/
127. http://www.youtube.com/watch?v=9zsqTqgBTk
128. http://www.arlingtoncemetery.net/terror.htm
129. http://www.patriotism.org/mlk/
130. http://www.biography.com/articles/Jesse-Jackson-9351181
131. http://www.cancer.gov/drugdictionary/?CdrID=39207
132. http://www.wrongdiagnosis.com/t/testicular_cancer/prognosis. htm
133. http://www.crimeandinvestigation.co.uk/crime-files/brinks-mat-bullion-heist/crime.html
134. http://www.imdb.com/title/tt0086687/
135. http://news.bbc.co.uk/onthisday/hi/dates/stories/january/27/ newsid_4046000/4046605.stm
136. http://www.history-of-rock.com/marvin_gaye.htm
137. http://www.nba.com/history/players/jordan_bio.html
138. http://www.biography.com/articles/Prince-9447278
139. http://prince.org/
140. http://www.missamerica.org/our-miss-americas/1980/1984.aspx
141. http://www.missamerica.org/our-miss-americas/1980/1984b.aspx
142. http://store.apple.com/us
143. http://www.northjersey.com/community/events/102600754_ Macintosh_Computer_Club.html
144. http://health.google.com/health/ref/AIDS
145. http://inventors.about.com/od/astartinventions/a/air_bags.htm
146. http://www.cdc.gov/mmwr/preview/mmwrhtml/00000596.htm
147. http://americanhistory.about.com/od/georgehwbush/a/ff_g_hw_ bush.htm
148. http://www.cnn.com/ALLPOLITICS/1996/conventions/ chicago/facts

149. http://www.gwu.edu/~nsarchiv/NSAEBB/NSAEBB272/
150. http://history1900s.about.com/od/1980s/a/flight103.htm
151. http://www.nytimes.com/1989/07/08/us/import-ban-on-assault-rifles-becomes-permanent.html
152. http://www.alaska.net/~awss/pws.html
153. http://www.exxonmobil.com/corporate/about _issues_valdez.aspx
154. http://www.azcentral.com/news/election/mccain/articles/2007/03/01/20070301mccainbio-chapter7.html
155. http://www.hyperhistory.net/apwh/bios/b1khomeini.htm
156. http://legal.web.aol.com/resources/legislation/comfraud.html
157. http://www.nasa.gov/columbia/home/index.html
158. http://www.prop1.org/history/2004/040806.typaper.lafayettepark.Abandon%20Quip.htm
159. http://nobelprize.org/nobel_prizes/peace/laureates/1993/klerk-bio.html
160. http://www.thelocal.de/national/20090920-22033.html
161. http://www.germanplaces.com/about- germany/history-east-and-west.html
162. http://www.sahistory.org.za/pages/ governance-projects/passive-resistance/1989.htm
163. http://www.globalsecurity.org/military/ops/just_cause.htm
164. http://www.foxnews.com/world/2010/06/28/ex-panamanian-dictator -manuel-noriega-goes-trial-france/
165. http://www.answers.com/topic/gulf-war
166. http://www.fas.org/news/un/iraq/sres/sres0678.htm
167. http://www.msnbc.msn.com/id/11971376/
168. http://www.hyperhistory.net/apwh/bios/b2gorbachevm.htm
169. http://nobelprize.org/alfred_nobel/
170. http://nobelprize.org/nobel_prizes/peace/laureates /1993/mandela- bio.html
171. http://www.biography.com/articles/John-Gotti-9542186
172. http://journals.lww.com/aidsonline/Citation/1991/03000/Statistics_from_the_World_Health _Organization_and.18.aspx
173. http://thecaucus.blogs.nytimes.com/2007/12/10/giuliani-on-homosexuality/
174. http://www.whitehouse.gov/about/presidents/georgehwbush
175. http://www.ada.gov/

176. http://clerk.house.gov/art_history/house_history/goldMedal.html
177. http://www.wordiq.com/definition/List_of_Heavyweight_Champions
178. http://www.heavyweights.co.uk/
179. http://www.fortunecity.com/marina/reach/435/windows.htm
180. http://www.ibiblio.org/pioneers/lee.html
181. http://www.imdb.com/name/nm0000637/183
182. http://wapedia.mobi/en/Results_of_the_1994_United_States_Figure_Skating_Championships
183. http://sports.espn.go.com/espn/espn25/story?page=moments/10
184. http://www.buttonmonkey.com/misc/maryfischer.html
185. http://www.nytimes.com/1996/01/14/weekinreview/ideas-trends-blame-global-warming-for-the-blizzard.html
186. http://www.investopedia.com/ask/answers/08/whitewater-scandal.asp
187. http://www.trutv.com/library/crime/terrorists_spies/terrorists/kaczynski/1.html
188. http://www.cato.org/pubs/pas/pa-262.html
189. http://www.fact-index.com/i/ir/iraq_disarmament_crisis.html
190. http://www.un.org/Depts/unscom/unscom.htm
191. http://www.stripes.com/news/r-r-facility-opens-in-republican-guard-club-1.12786
192. http://www.historyguy.com/no-fly_zone_war.html
193. http://www.globalsecurity.org/military/ops/desert_strike.htm
194. http://www.conservapedia.com/United_States_presidential_election,_1996
195. http://www.wnd.com/news/article.asp?ARTICLE_ID=60001
196. http://www.fact-index.com/1/19/1996.html
197. http://www.motherteresa.org/
198. http://www.biography.com/notorious/crimefiles.do?catId=259458&action=view&profileId=260625
199. http://www.justice.gov/oip/foia_updates/Vol_XVII_4/page2.htm
200. http://www.trutv.com/library/crime/notorious_murders/famous/ramsey/index_1.html
201. http://www.royal.gov.uk/
202. http://www.trutv.com/library/crime/notorious_murders/famous/menendez/brothers_6.html

203. http://www.animalresearch.info/en/medical/timeline/Dolly
204. http://www.olympic.org/en/content/Olympic-Games/All-Past-Olympic-Games/Summer/Atlanta-1996/
205. http://www.waymarking.com/waymarks/WM24K3_Centennial_Olympic_Park_Bombing_Atlanta_Georgia
206. http://www.cnn.com/ALLPOLITICS/1996/conventions/chicago/facts/tidbits/chicago.history.shtml
207. http://wallstreetpit.com/44551-government-shutdown-talk
208. http://spark-korea.org/
209. http://www.justice.gov.za/trc/
210. http://www.infoplease.com/spot/osamabinladen.html#axzz0zYHHmrUy
211. http://www.npr.org/templates/story/story.php?storyId=1434187
212. http://www.microsoft.com/presspass/exec/billg/
213. http://whatreallyhappened.com/RANCHO/POLITICS/OK/ok.html
214. http://www.royalty.nu/Europe/England/Windsor/Diana.html
215. http://support.microsoft.com/kb/234762
216. http://www.apple.com/
217. http://inventors.about.com/library/inventors/bllaptop.htm
218. http://www.everymac.com/systems/apple/powermac_g4/index-powermac-g4.html
219. http://www.members.tripod.com/~vanessawest/columbine-4.html
220. http://www.nndb.com/people/061/000113719/
221. http://www.imdb.com/title/tt0120915/
222. http://www.lib.utexas.edu/taro/tslac/40078/tsl-40078.html
223. http://www.census.gov/main/www/popclock.html
224. http://www.hurricanekatrina.com/
225. http://americanhistory.about.com/od/georgewbush/a/ff_g_w_bush.htm
226. http://www.globalsecurity.org/wmd/world/dprk/nuke.htm
227. http://www.un.org/apps/news/story.asp?NewsID=20255&Cr=ki-moon&Cr1
228. http://www.globalsecurity.org/security/profiles/islamic_state_of_iraq.htm
229. http://www.globalsecurity.org/military/world/iraq/saddam.htm
230. http://www.hrcr.org/hottopics/iraqitribunal.html